CAT DISH GIN

Have More Fun in Life, Sex,
Parenting, and Aging Through
Self-Care Quickies.

Heather Curlee Novak

*a little powder room.
reading in 2 page bites.
messy life & humor.
xo Heather*

ISBN-13: 9798327859517
ISBN-10: 1477123456

Cover design by Anastasia Herasymchuk
Library of Congress Control Number: 2018675309
Printed in the United States of America

"I thought such awful thoughts that I cannot even say them out loud because they would make Jesus want to drink gin straight out of the cat dish."

ANNE LAMOTT

ACKNOWLEDGEMENTS

A jillion years ago, my dear friend, Jean DeWinter, challenged me to write a radio commentary for our local NPR station as a creative adventure. I never submitted the paltry scrabble I wrote down then, but years later, I had a vivid dream, which I wrote down in essay form and sent to Lee Burdorf at WVPE. He invited me to record it, which aired on NPR around 2009.

Incredibly, April Lidinsky, the woman in charge of the local "Michiana Chronicles" show, enjoyed the essay and invited me to join the team of writers. I have been writing these lifestyle Chronicles ever since. April is a fiercely funny feminist I have had the privilege of knowing for almost twenty years. She invited me onto a public radio stage and gave me a microphone for my thoughts. She saw me as a woman and showed me that my words had value to a greater audience.

Without Jean and April, I would not have the life of words I enjoy today.

Thanks to Lee Burdorf and Tony Krabill for the

technical shenannigans of recording me all these years.

Thanks to all the Michiana Chroniclers for supporting my pieces alongside your great works.

I want to smooch with thankfulness my husband John, daughters Portia and Libby, and all the friends and family that appear in these stories, some named, some anonymous. Thank you for sharing your lives with me and allowing me to share 'us' on air (and now in print.) What we say and do matters, and it makes the world better.

CONTENTS

FEEDING WILLARD

This is how I was told to prepare for parenthood: Carve a one-inch circular hole into a pumpkin, tie it to a rope hanging from your ceiling, and start swinging it. Take applesauce on a spoon and try to stuff as much of it as possible into the moving target or else it will scream. Tada! Feeding our daughter isn't that bad most days, but I learned a whole new sense of appreciation for it when my Uncle Frank visited us from Colorado.

Uncle Frank spent a great deal of his daily free time for years caring for my Grandfather. Frank would feed Grandpa Willard at least one meal most days. They would go to restaurants where Grandpa would drink too much and fall asleep before eating much of whatever it was he liked that day. The whole excursion would take hours because Grandpa Willard was wheelchair-bound and needed a special shuttle to travel anywhere. Despite all the trouble of arranging transportation, nurses, and equipment, Uncle Frank made sure Grandpa also got to 'Dreamland', his little cabin in the rocky mountains once or twice a year. Frank got Grandpa loaded onto a Ferris wheel, to the opera, ball games, and yes, to many, many restaurants. My Uncle took exquisite loving care of him for about eight years before

Grandpa Willard died in the Spring of 2009.

When Uncle Frank was here visiting us, he fed our six-month-old baby Portia several meals and shared how similar it was to feeding Willard. Her eager anticipation was evident in the banging of her little palms on the highchair tray. How she would grin and then open her mouth like a baby bird lunging towards the spoon. Frank said Grandpa Willard ate his meals with the same zeal most days. Frank scraped dribbled food from Portia's chin, and his father's too. Both of them had fairly soft, bland culinary options offered to them when they seemed more interested in a big juicy steak.

As we talked about how similar feeding a baby and an old person was, we stumbled over the meaning of life. Or at least we discovered one of them. The meaning of life can be found in eating, consuming, and devouring. And not just devouring food. Every one of us needs to eat to survive, but there is so much more.

We consume energy, knowledge, time, space, experience, and love. We make and use energy doing everyday tasks like getting out of bed or turning on the coffee pot. We devour books and words and moments that teach us new things. We drink mountain air and river water through our noses, breathing deep breaths that sustain us. We thrive on experiences throughout our lives and become the people we are through having those things occur in front of us. We consume love and get drunk in the amorous cocoon we find ourselves in. We are in love with our lover, in love with our children, loving our friends, and sometimes even ourselves when we let our guard down.

Sometimes, as in feeding a Baby, the best part of the meal dribbles forgotten down our chin. Sometimes, as in feeding Willard, we get drunk on all the options of life, missing the select few bits of deliciousness we would have savored. Sometimes we awaken at the table of life and realize we have gorged ourselves on junk food, leaving behind the morsels that would have truly sustained us.

We eat and dribble knowledge down our chins as we try to weigh what we learn against what we believe. We share bites of it with the people around us to test their reactions. Sometimes they show us what we thought was sweet tastes bitter. When we consume with another it often adjusts the flavor we enjoy. Eating food and living life with others adds to the sweetness.

The best of these times is when our consumption turns into our giving. When what we take in becomes better when we give it out. When we know that sharing with another brings them peace or joy or fulfillment-- that makes the meaning in our life. When our being loved by another creates in us a softer heart, a more patient spirit, a more giving soul. Life is better when we turn these gifts back out again in our everyday lives. Every one of us consumes, what do we give back? I would like to become more unselfish and giving, like my Uncle Frank. I'm going to spend some time this week considering who else I can feed or share a meal with. Are you free for dinner?

RESPONSIBLE HAPPINESS

Are we happiest when we take responsibility for our lives, or when we shirk our duties and goof off instead? I for one am DELIGHTED to not wash dinner dishes, even though The Fly Lady says I always should.* I like not being responsible and sitting on my couch with John binge-watching Netflix until we go to bed.

I wake and stretch and give thanks for the day and waltz smack into a nasty dirty kitchen. Crumbs, smudges, dirty French press. Sink full of gooey grossness. My mood stalls and fizzles as I begin to mutter and clean up. Then I make breakfast for our family and there are MORE dishes. Gah! I guess I'll look at Facebook and avoid it all. Till Lunch. Dishes are still there and now I am flinging more into the sink! GAHHH!!!!

When I avoid being the grown-up and taking responsibility for my home, things, and jobs, it may feel good for a moment. But I still have to do it at some point. Oh! And it negatively affects my mood the entire time I am avoiding it. I try to remind myself that not washing the dishes, folding the clothes, or taking care of work will weigh on me even while I am trying to relax and have fun. I am happier and more satisfied when I take care of the responsibility FIRST and then relax(Most of the time).

Some friends and I have been watching this Andy Stanley series online called "Taking Responsibility for Your Life", and that is part of where these ideas festered. One hard point he makes is that when I choose NOT to take responsibility for something, SOMEBODY has to do it for me.

Stanley has this whole schtick where he says we should simplify our lives by asking the person who will have to step in and be responsible for us in advance. Like I'd say to my husband John "John, I'm too lazy to do the dishes, will you do them for me so you do not have to deal with me feeling overwhelmed and grouchy in the morning?" We even started using this with the kids to interesting effect: "Portia, please ask me to pick that towel up off the floor because you don't want to take care of your things." Instead of just picking it up for her.

I've been trying to improve in this area even if it means I had to wash the dishes before sitting down here to write this for you fine people this morning. I remind myself I am NEVER going to WANT to do the dishes. I will probably never WANT to fold clothes or rake leaves or what have you. Now I have to go keep the kids alive some more. Enjoy taking care of your responsibilities today. And have some SATISFIED FUN!

BORED

Are you bored in your life? Do you seem to have lots of moments where you ask yourself, "Well, what now?" or "Well, what's on TV now?" I've had this conversation with a few people recently where they admit boredom and I stare blankly trying to comprehend the word they have just used. Boredom? I think the last time I was bored was maybe twenty years ago as a teenager! My guess is we are required to be bored for most of the teen years, or we aren't allowed to get to the drinking age, there would be no purpose. We would also never be motivated to move on with our lives and go to college, get a job, and have adventures. Then again, maybe not. From time to time we all could stand a good hard look at our lives and how we are living them, to be sure we are getting the most out of our breathing above-ground days.

I read recently in a parenting magazine that author Donald Miller wanted to live a better and more interesting life. A biography of his life was in the works but they told him his life wasn't interesting enough! He gave up TV for a year and biked across the country to liven himself up, just for starters. I have several friends who do that kind of grueling trip and I like admiring them from a distance. I'm not doing that.

I'm expecting a new baby almost any day now, so at nine months pregnant a walk around the block is pretty close to a cross-country bike ride for me. I have plenty of adventure trying to keep my husband and toddler alive and happy most days. Even though boredom is not a familiar experience for me, these conversations and the Donald Miller article about living a better life have engaged me and made me think about how I spend my time.

Before having a family, I used to work outside of the home as a sales and service trainer. I used to speak in front of groups of professionals, at church retreats, and classes. I used to dress up all pretty in clothes that were stylish and wore little heels instead of Birkenstocks or Crocs and my hair wasn't accessorized by the lone bobby pin to keep bangs at bay. I was engaged in a professional, vibrant world of learning and teaching and reaching new goals. It is different now as a stay-at-home mom. I cannot say it isn't as exciting. You try to keep a toddler from falling downstairs fourteen times a day or from grabbing knives off the kitchen counter when she's grown six inches overnight and tell me it isn't...exciting. I'm so grateful to be home with our daughter and to be the person learning alongside her each day, but I can see where there could be more.

My Mother died when I was thirteen years old, and I believe it's that experience that taught me the early lesson that life doesn't last. From this lesson, I've known all my life that there are lots of great things to do with my time and only a limited amount of that time to do them all. This core of my being has shaped both my younger professional life and my life as a stay-at-home mama. I try to seek out the most interesting options, the life-engaging and affirming ways to spend our time, and I think this rescues me from potential boredom.

I have lived a life on fire and have very few regrets. I have lived in Chicago, Colorado, California, and Indiana. I've swing danced, painted, written, acted, gone on political rally bus trips to Washington, seen movies alone, snowshoed, water skied, geocached, eaten dinner in the bathtub, made candles, drank champagne for breakfast on the front porch, cooked up fabulous new food and total kitchen disasters including flaming bagels. I have read garbage books, naughty books, highbrow books, and educational books. I've volunteered for homeless shelters, deaf communities, disabled adults, and churches. I've driven cross country many times, raised two dogs from pups, angsted through mix tapes, finished college late, took jobs too big for me, worked jobs too small for me, and smiled at strangers regularly.

Now in my life as a Mama, I go to every story hour, take my daughter to play dates, zoos, museums, and construction sites, and do my best to show her the world with all its details large and small. I'm not trying to shield her from boredom, I think it has its place in childhood. I just want her to learn how easy it can be to engage herself in a bigger life through even the smallest things. I want her to, like me, live her life in reality, not on screen through TV or the computer. I want her to benefit from the life lessons I had to learn the hard way...isn't that every parent's sweetest dream?

If they were writing the biography of your life would it say you could recount every episode of LOST and worked hard at the job you hated but that is about it? What is on your bucket list? What adventures are you waiting to have? If your adventure is too big to be feasible right now what are smaller versions of it you could dance with? Don't be bored! You have too much to do. I encourage you to fill your life with people who matter deeply to you. I can never say enough about volunteering your time and skill as an effective lifebuilder. If you have been struggling with the status quo of daily doings I hope that sharing with you some of how I have lived my life out loud will set off some bells and get you off the proverbial couch into LIFE! None of us have enough days in our life to spend them chin in hand brooding and wishing there were more. There is MUCH more; get up and find it!

DEATH &
GUACAMOLE

I made guacamole today. I made guacamole today to celebrate life. I made guacamole as a ritual with which to honor a death. A young woman I have never met died yesterday. I learned this when I dropped off some books at my friend Stephanie's house. I found her beautiful that morning in the unmade-up way of the stay-at-home, work-at-home mama. Radiant skin, long brunette hair falling in waves loose and beautiful around her shoulders, a full skirt, and a tired smile on her face.

I didn't know until later she might have been crying. She had just found out her good friend Samantha lost a battle with cancer at twenty-eight years old. Samantha helped her set up the "Listen To Your Mother" show I got to be in and Stephanie directed it. Listen to Your Mother was how Stephanie and I had first met.

So we stood at her front door talking about life and death and naked Saturday (which you would understand if you have small children, or if you watched our "Listen to Your Mother" Show on YouTube.) We exchanged some books. We talked about faith, churches and open-mindedness. We admired her daughter, spinning to show off her princess skirt. I stayed on the front porch step, eyeing my two daughters dozing in the car.

I didn't try to soothe what I imagined was a very heavy heart. I felt embarrassed because I wasn't sure if I got to meet Samantha. I was uncomfortable not knowing how to react to the death of someone I might or might not know who was younger than I was and left many people without enough time with her. So I made guacamole.

I was inspired to hit the kitchen after I looked at Stephanie's blog www.adventuresinbabywearing.com to see what she might have written about this loss. She simply wrote that she lay on the grass in her yard and felt the sun on her face. That when she got hungry she went in and made guacamole and ate it straight out of the mixing bowl. This is all she wrote that day. I knew she was writing about grief. She was writing about how precious little moments are. She was missing a friend's future and what their relationship might have become if years lost could have progressed. She wasn't making guacamole; she was celebrating life and reversing death.

I had an avocado in my vegetable drawer. I had tortilla chips in the pantry. I had an onion, a lime, garlic cloves, cumin, tomatoes, and sea salt. I too made guacamole. I celebrated life and revered death and missed a woman I may have never met.

JUNE 2016

I've been busy sleeping in and enjoying the leisure of summer this past week. I have had a relaxed schedule but have not been reading my bible, praying much or working on the two devotionals I really get a lot out of. I was in the car solo driving to the WVPE NPR station in Elkhart to record three pieces for Michiana Chronicles when 'ol Padnah got my attention. Yes, yes, I thought, we should spend some of this good quality time together! I changed the station from NPR to look for a worship station to set the tone for our time together.

I found a station with a pastor preaching about some scripture where Paul was speaking. I settled into it until he said something about us being sinners. Yes, I agree with that, and continue to be aware of how my sin, although God has forgiven it, continues to affect me within my life. I sin, I have sin, I am a sinner. Yes. Then the pastor went on to say something like "We are all sinners every one of us and we are evil and there is no good in us, nothing worthy without the saving grace of Jesus Christ."

WHOA.

"That is theologically incorrect, Lord!" I said to the empty car. "No! This is wrong...sinners yes, nothing good, no." I felt strongly in my soul that God was getting my attention. Human beings are made in the image of God. They are good, absolutely wonderful in fact. Scriptures say we are fearfully and wonderfully made. Yes we have that selfishness of sin and yes we make poor choices... some of us may be evil, but all of us are modeled after God and meant to live beautiful lives of love and passion no matter our circumstances.

I turned the radio off as I leaned into the moment and drove along the highway swigging Starbucks Pikes Place coffee with cream. Writing this very book came into my mind again when I hadn't given it a moment's thought for the past year. I felt bashful about it. There are so many incredible writers in the world, my little bits here couldn't be published, it wouldn't matter if I would want them too. In my prayer time in the car, God asked me how I thought I knew more than he did?

I knew one thing at that moment: Every person alive should KNOW they matter in this Kardashian Esque-social-media-live-beyond-your-means-desperately-   trying-to-fill-our-God-shaped-hole world. Who was I to keep someone from reading these words and connecting with God in a way they hadn't before? It is not my job to worry about the value of these words, these faith filled moments in time. It is up to me only to write them out as well as I can and float them out into the universe. God will be certain the right people, be they few or many, read my heart and see God's heart instead. I have decided today to get out of the

way and let God love me in these words. He is
loving you too. You are wonderful, you are loved,
and you matter. Who do you know who also needs
to know the truth about themselves?

IDEAS FOR A PERFECT MARRIAGE

My husband John and I just had our five year anniversary. He is incredible and God's best gift to my life, even over my children. (And oh! I love my girls so much.) He meets my weakness with his strength and his life choices are usually inline with mine. He is selfless more often than I am. He is smart, wise and pretty darn handsome to boot.

So this got me thinking about how other folks could have a perfect marriage.

It is simple really: Be a Perfect Mate! Ok, Ok stop laughing...I don't want you to choke on your breakfast there. I am as far from perfect as it gets, so please do not take me literally. What I mean by "be a perfect mate" is look at what you want in your spouse, and then consider what he or she might want in their mate.

A funny thing happens when a husband or wife starts being the sort of spouse they want. Many times they will start getting the kind of spouse they want.

Here are five tips to get closer to relationship bliss.

1) Do Not Expect Them to Be Your Everything

A spouse is a big deal in our lives. We women especially like to put any neediness we have on the man we love. We want them to make us feel smart and pretty and important endlessly.

I finally realized that John was a real person who got grouchy or tired or bored or distracted. I could not base the temperature of our relationship on how he reacted to me any given day. He doesn't criticize me when I look like a homeless person and haven't showered for a day. Or Two. This is priceless in a husband. But the flip side is, he won't exactly do cartwheels and layer on compliments when I do put on a little mascara. So I tell myself how foxy I am and have my girlfriends to admire my preening. I do not expect him to be my personal validation.

2) You are Not the Boss of Them

This one is really hard for me because I know the best thing for him and the right way to do everything related to our home, our life, our social adventures and our children. Nagging doesn't work. The word itself sounds horrible, why do anything that could even be called nagging? Your Darling is a grown up person over 21 with a driver's license. They don't want or need you to tell them what to do or remind them(however helpful you mean to be) about what needs to be done. They might not do what you think needs to be done and the world will not end. Even if you are right. If you only want something done your way, then do it yourself! Offer your mate respect as an adult to live their own life within your marriage.

3) Ask Them What Matters Most

I used to assume my husband wanted me in makeup and nice clothes with a gorgeous dinner over which I told him hilarious and engaging stories from my day and the world at large. I thought scheduling fun activities throughout the week like art openings, concerts, fish suppers and local festivals was adding to his daily joy. I was wrong. I get filled up by activity but my husband gets drained by it! When I finally asked him what I could do to make his life better, he said I could schedule less stuff in a week. Turns out I become a bit of a stress ball with all that extra debris on our calendar, and (imagine that!) he doesn't love it. Ask your spouse what fills them up, you may be surprised.

4) Date your Mate

I don't mean just make time for date night although that is very helpful in creating a strong, happy marriage. I mean act like you did when you were dating. We get married and then take for granted our spouse's presence in our lives. We yawn at their work stories, glaze over when she acts silly and we stop dressing up or doing our hair every time we see him...because we see them all of the time.

Many affairs start simply because the person doesn't feel important or valued by their spouse anymore. Someone new finds him fascinating and so he becomes fascinating and is in turn fascinated with the new woman. Can we be the new woman? Surprise him with a night off to go out by himself or with friends instead of putting kids to bed. Look at her, really look at her when she talks. Remember that everyone wants to feel important, and your spouse should be important to you.

5) The fifth tip towards having the perfect marriage

Make the decision to appreciate your marriage right now. Your choices make the difference in your life. Choose to enjoy your life and relationship now, just as it is.

LIVE WELL

Our family motto is "Live Well". It is short, sweet and difficult to do. It can be tricky in a day filled with redundant tasks like laundry and laundry and laundry and then washing two hundred and forty-six dishes to do anything other than sink into a cozy chair with my laptop and spend an hour on Facebook. Or Pinterest. Or Twitter. Or Netflix. Or Ravelry. Or ...well you can see spending my free time is pretty easy. Or is it?

For most of us, screen time is the default for our free time. That and eating. Or eating in front of a screen, mostly the TV screen! YES! Now, TV isn't the only bad guy, all the Internet sites and games are fun to use up our time, too.

I think unwinding in front of a screen or gathering information through it is perfectly fine to a point. I want to choose that intentionally, instead of just slipping into it because it is easy. It is so easy.

In order to make our family motto of "Live Well" a reality, I need to be aware of how I currently live. I took some time to jot down a few things that refreshed me and made me happy.

Some were small happy, some were huge happy, each of them made a difference in how I felt on any given day.

One thing that makes me happy is drinking a cup of coffee that is hot the first time. Usually I reheat it more than a few times each morning before I get to it. I love the hammock I got for Mother's Day. I have enjoyed the bliss of a hammock since I was a little kid sticking my legs through the rope holes and swinging wildly. I love a new project. I do not love finishing a new project, but the thrill of starting one is huge for me. I also love good food. I cook and bake and really enjoy cooking for family, friends and myself.

In order to live well, I need to make time for what makes me happy and refreshed. Sometimes I am so tired at the end of the day spending energy or brainpower to choose something other than collapsing on the couch seems daunting. I believe that to make the most of my life, daily and for the long haul, I cannot operate on default and slide through my days without a long term plan. If I want to operate with a financial budget, I have to keep track of my money and plan how to best spend it. The same is true of my life. I have discovered that once I began to pursue a more fulfilling free time adventure it was more than worth the effort. But it does take effort!

There is a knitting group on Monday nights

I love going to and listening to the chatter. I am unusually quiet since I do not know the women well and that is refreshing for me. Most weeks it is easier to just sit and watch TV with my hubby after the girls are in bed. It takes effort to walk or bike downtown to sit and knit with those ladies, but it is always worth it. Always.

Biking places instead of driving, either solo or trailering my two tots behind me...that is another choice I want to make in order to live well. When I don't use a car I feel good about myself, have less stress, help the environment and see a lot more things with my girls than if we were whizzing by in the car. Once it was a huge gnarly tree with a strange web of bare branches more like a bush than a tree-tree. About head height was a plastic charm bracelet dangling there. I got such a chuckle out of that. I am easy to amuse, I suppose. That is a choice too!

Naming and Choosing what refreshes me helps us to be more mindful about how I spend my free time. I can so easily loose an hour rabbit trailing through the internet or watching reruns on Netflix. I'm still only halfway through Desperate Housewives, but do I really want to dedicate a zillion hours to watching fake people live fake lives? Or could I finally get de-stressed and physically fit instead? Could I use that time to finish writing my book? Could I make so many memories geocaching and playing and wandering with my family that we cannot remember how we used to spend our time? Live Well. Short and sweet and hard to do. I'll bet there are other good family mottos on Pinterest...or maybe I will keep writing-- and living--my own.

THE POOP IS
THE SAME

Potty training is a venture every parent undertakes at some point before their kidlets go off to college...or kindergarten. Over the past year as my husband, toddler daughter and I have yelled, wept, bribed, cursed, sighed and laughed over our version of housebreaking a human, I have seen an interesting thing. (Yes, it is going to be interesting. This will be interesting even for those of you who have no interest whatsoever in the goings on or the going on the potty action with children.) So listen up: Potty Training is like Working in the following situations:

Situation One: Everybody does it. Everyone works during their life like it or not. Just like everyone is at one time or another involved in potty training. Even if you aren't signing up for parenthood, your folks aimed your tuckus in the porcelain throne direction more than a few times, I bet.

Situation Two: Potty training a hungry tired angry distracted annoyed devious lying laughing toddler is about what your average work meeting looks like. (You are chuckling because you know this to be true.) A staff meeting in any business setting always has a herding of the cats element to it. Or in the case of my point, a herding of the heiny to the potty element to it. Potty Training, Working!

Situation Three: You can lead a horse to water, (WAIT. That could be gross, never mind.)

Situation Four: Even though you want people to be responsible for their own mess, sometimes you are the one-man cleaning crew.

Situation Five: Sometimes in your work life, you think your idea is AWESOME. You think you have nailed it and you are set up for advancement, a raise and the corner office. But then you step back and notice...your aim wasn't so great after all.

Situation Six: Sometimes at work there is a line for the bathroom and you have to wait a bit. Or you need a bit of....privacy...and so want to claim the bathroom all to yourself privately. Potty training is the same except the bathroom is always needed as soon as you have availed yourself of it, and no, they are not willing to wait in a line.

Situation Seven: Dressing for success is common in business. When it comes to potty training, undressing for success is the way of it. (Frankly, undressing for success can be common for work and potty training, come to think of it.)

Situation Eight: Potty Training is like working in an office because sometimes what starts out as a team building event ends up with everyone in tears sitting on the floor together. Except in potty training there is also hugging. And M&Ms. Not likely to be found in an office. Well, maybe the M&Ms?

Situation Nine: At work there are countless occasions when someone does something so basic and expected for their job but still wants a big kudos. In Potty Training, Someone also does something so basic and expected and still wants a big kudos for it.

Situation Ten: Finally, in both working and potty training every day the poop is the same and you are often the one in the middle of it...but eventually everything gets cleaned up and put to right and tomorrow is a whole new day. With clean underpants!

PLEASURE CACHE

Pleasure is a funny thing. It can show up to stretch with a feline nonchalance into unexpected moments. This morning I stretched before I got out of bed. It was delicious. I forget how much pleasure can be found in a slow leisurely full body stretch. Later in the day, walking in winter sunshine with my friends was pure pleasure. All three of us pushed our tiny people in strollers hoping they would doze in the sun and fresh air. We had no agenda or particular destination until I suggested we go after a geocache.

We are mothers. We fill many of the stereotypes of the un-showered unkempt un-private bathroom time many people have of motherhood. We struggle for alone time and live for naptime. The baby's nap, not ours. Well, usually not ours. If we could dream and indulge in pleasures, I think it would be us all alone and it would probably be quiet. Or loud, it could be loud music that makes us smile, that makes us feel a little naughtier like when we were younger and more careless. We would probably chat with a friend or make a craft. Most Mamas wouldn't geocache.

Geocaching is a worldwide treasure hunt for worthless things in surprising places. I bet you there is a geocache within ten miles of your home right now. In the Michiana area there are maybe several hundred alone. Enough to keep you busy hunting. They can be a puzzle where you gather information to solve it. They can be a container as small as your fingertip or as big as a barrel hidden somewhere that cachers can find and re-hide again and again. Geocaching.com is a great resource if you are curious and want to know more.

When I was single I would go caching constantly. I would adventure out at night at all hours to be the first to find a new geocache. I even went out in winter snow because it is easier to find something when you can follow other people's tracks. I spent entire days hunting for caches alone and with friends. I found over two hundred and placed several of my own. Now I do not cache. I have these two small people to lug in and out of the car. I don't drag my children through the woods or bushwack in brambles. I do not cache. I miss it.

Until I got a smartphone, I also had technological stumbles. But now. Oh! Now I can turn my phone on when I have some time to kill and search out a nearby geocache. I have taken my husband and older daughter and shared the thrill of the find with them. And today I took my mama friends.

We pushed our strollers through mud. We appointed one of us to watch all three strollers while the other two of us foraged. We wandered. We laughed. And we found it. A peanut butter jar wrapped in camouflage tape with a log book inside to sign our names. None of the trinkets interested us so we put it all back as we found it. We smiled and laughed at ourselves and I think the two of them will look again for caches. We enjoyed the unexpected fun of hidden treasure and instead of mamas with great responsibilities, we were kids again. Kids playing in the mud, in the bushes. The pleasure of a surprisingly warm day and a hidden treasure were ours. And the small people in those strollers? They were stretching and sleeping in the sun.

UGLY PEOPLE

Yep, you are ugly. You woke up this morning and took one look at yourself and know you are ugly. I thought, since you said it first, I would share a few muddled thoughts I was having on this very topic as I rolled out of bed this morning. As I get older, I take more time with my appearance most days. I wear makeup most days. I find fault with myself most days.

You too? Oh great, we will get along just fine. You have cellulite on the *front* of your thighs? Awesome, me too. Your hair is fabulous when you don't need to go anywhere or see anyone, but goes haywire when you want to feel pretty? Yup, me too. You yell at your kids when they are just being kids but happen to get on your very last nerve with their high pitched 'puppy' barking? Yep.

Ugly comes in a lot of different forms. We usually focus on the face and body, but ugly sneaks out of our personalities too. That might be the hardest to admit.

Everyone is Ugly, some just hide it better! Good looking parents, expensive clothes or beauty products, dimmer lights...whatever the lovely folks have that you don't simply hides what we all have: ugly. Some people hide their inner ugly by leaving a situation before it shows. Or counting to ten very slowly. I am teaching my little girls to take deep 'yoga breaths' and count to ten when they are upset. I want them to be able to learn things I didn't about leaving their ugly hidden when possible.

It isn't always possible to hide your ugly. I had to spend some time with one of my favorite folks this week. I missed her so much. And thus we squeezed in a quick play/lunch date right after I worked out. Folks, I was ugly. I smelled bad and wore my lycra shorts over there. Those suckers don't go anywhere but the gym and thru the 'hood on runs. But I needed my friend, so I showed her my ugly. She was pretty enough to say she couldn't even smell me.

Be sure to find or make friends who will see that you are ugly but won't admit it. Or if they do, they help freshen you a bit! And it is ok for your ugly to show. Your friendships will deepen when you are authentic about how you feel inside and outside. When you are real about your own struggles, you give people around you the freedom to share their struggles too. Somebody may need that permission more than you know.

I have some things I do, for when I am UGLY.

1) Ask God to remind me of my beauty, and then

get outside in nature!

2) Do something with my body; exercise, cuddle my girls and read, drink a smoothie or juice veggies, shower and primp a bit.

3) Put on bright red lipstick. Even with a bathrobe.

4) Call or write to a friend telling them about their beauty and how they bless my life.

5) Read great books like Captivating by John & Stasi Eldridge, Made to Crave by Lysa Terkhurst or something else that gives me a point to start over with how I see myself.

6) Paint some TRUTH CARDS from Brave Girls Club to encourage another woman.

7) Eat something. Sorry, shouldn't be here, right, but it is true. Cheese popcorn, Unreal Candy, Oh! How you make me feel lovely.

8) Get thankful. This trick has been an oldie but a goodie. I write down or speak out loud every little silly thing I am grateful for, from hot coffee to a cushy seat to sit on while I'm sulking. It works every time.

9) Pray for others who do not have the luxury of worrying about cellulite or wrinkles. I give thanks that I have a blessed life full of family, good health, intelligence, beauty and freedom. Any second everything could change, and I could see how pitiful my small vain woes truly are.

10) SMILE! Your brain and body do not know the difference between real happiness and a forced smile. Start smiling at others, but especially yourself in the mirror, and you will see your beauty.

P.S. YOU look wonderful to me!

TALES OF A HORROR STORY BASEMENT

Have you ever seen a movie, like a thriller or a horror film where you KNOW that person shouldn't go in the basement?   They kind of write the scene that way to get your adrenaline pumping. Going into that basement just means they will never come back out of it. I have one of these basements. In my dark, damp, ugly basement, Things Get Lost. We call it Storing Stuff, but really, if we are honest, we just Lose Stuff in our basement. Down the rickety 'Needs Paint' stairs are mildewed walls and a cold bare floor. (Is it just cold, or is it wet too? I often idly wonder, but not for long.) My horror story basement stands guard over all our sentimental crap and extra house decorations. I suppose one could also do laundry in it. If one was into that kind of thing.

I've tried to reclaim the basement. I lured some gal pals down with cheap wine to sit like high school girls and brainstorm options. We didn't do anything, just talked. And drank wine. We priced waterproofing the whole damp thing. We have shop vacced water out many times. My husband may have cleaned out...umm, not water from the sewer drain. Once. We know where to put things (dry floor) and where not to (*wet floor*) put them.

In the act of storing a downsized dinner table in the basement, I now have a craft area. The table is covered with a plastic tablecloth to protect it from paint and glue. It is usually covered with boxes and bins of craft debris. If all the lights are turned on and my girls and I are working together, it feels almost safe to be down there. But if I am alone...well, that is why the laundry is always not done. Because I am scared to be in the basement. Right? I'm not lazy, it's self preservation!

One time I fought some mildew on one basement wall so the kids could have one sacred place to play Down There. This is for when I am doing my semi annual ironing pile purge. I put an area rug down and painted the wall with kilz paint. It looked inviting enough for them to spend a little time, but not alone. Never Alone! We leave some toys down there and since they see them so rarely it is like getting new toys!

There is one thing about my basement that does lure me, on occasion. Besides the deep freezer and the chocolate I hide by John's workbench. It is cool down there. As our summer days heat up and get muggier and muggier, the basement lures me with its cool damp floors and chilly air. When it is

80 degrees upstairs, just standing on the landing the temperature will drop at least ten degrees. Free air-conditioning! If you make it back out alive.

Recently I went down there to move the laundry along. It felt so cool and wonderful I lingered. The girls wandered down. I straightened some piles. I folded the laundry there on the craft table. I looked around for more work to do, more reasons to stay in the cool air. My eyes fell on the drawers I kept random crafts in. My gaze traveled to the cast off baker's rack we now use to store dog towels and Costco toilet paper. I began to form a plan. I knew what to do to stay in the basement a little longer.

I went quickly upstairs and grabbed the label maker from the office cabinet. Back down to the basement again. Friends, I labeled everything in sight! I brainstormed, organized and punched more letters in to label something else. I labeled like a madwoman. I may have laughed in delight as I put things where they should go instead of wherever they had landed. I moved things I needed to use more often to easier places. I knew labeling areas, bins and drawers would help me to have a place for everything and everything in its place. I was on fire. I was a crazed labeling lunatic.

I was so excited about the labeling and organizing; I realized I was the only scary thing in my horror story basement. Seriously: who gets that jazzed about labels?   Who gets high on organizing a basement?

We get a lot of hot, humid days in Indiana. After the impact I saw in just an hour with the label maker, I may keep going. I may find some lost things Down There. I may reclaim another wall for my children to play near. I may even think about painting those basement stairs. Heck if I use enough labels, the basement may waterproof itself!   Do you want to come down into my basement?   C'mon...it is so nice and cool and organized down there....c'mon, it's ok. Don't forget to bring your labels.

GARBAGE FOOD

Today I sat down to a nice pile of garbage for lunch. I didn't eat with Oscar the Grouch. I'm not talking tin cans and banana peels goat-eating-garbage scenario, I'm talking about the drive through. The golden arches, the bell made of tacos, the redheaded square burger stepchild or the laughable king. Fast Food is garbage food: why do I delight in it so?

I never cared much about what I ate as a single girl. Popcorn for dinner, McDonald's cheeseburgers and fries far too often. Now that I am older I have read too much, learned too much and aged too much to eat garbage food without thought. I still eat it, but not as often and not without various levels of regret. It started with the movie "Supersize Me" by Morgan Spurlock and the disgusting fact that a McDonald's cheeseburger and fries today will look the same in one month or longer.

Now I have two children and that journey from pregnancy to being 100% responsible for feeding other people has again reshaped my view of food. My husband and I listened to Michael Pollan's <u>In Defense of Food</u> as a book on audio on our way out to Colorado last year. You need thirty hours in the car to get through that sucker but it is worth it. His newer book <u>Food Rules</u> is more direct and even comes in an illustrated version. He talks about "real food" versus "fake food". Pollan says eat all the junk food you want, just make it yourself! He suggests we avoid any food product that has more than five ingredients because it is more likely to be a "food like" food item rather than an actual food.

This book changed my husband and I, and thankfully at the same time. We still eat garbage food, but we know that is what we are doing and so choose it less often. He takes his lunch to work most days and I bring snacks with me everywhere lest hunger should give me an excuse to "drive thru".

Yet I still Drive Thru. When I should keep right on "driving past" I don't. We don't go inside to eat either. A fast food restaurant is more a side note as we drive somewhere; it is never the destination. It is food designed to eat easily in a car. Food designed to eat in a hurry. To eat guiltily? I feel guilty feeding my two year old daughter McDonald's. It's marginally ok if I put it into my body but she has little choice. What I put in front of her is what she eats.

As we drive home eating steaming hot French fries, I think of our full fridge at home. It contains whole grain mac & cheese, leftover from scratch split pea soup, scalloped taters and ham. I could quickly produce almond butter sandwiches, cheese and crackers and fruit. Healthy lunch was easily had in our home, yet I cruised through the good 'ol drive thru. I have a lusty desire for the sugar-salt-fat trifecta and only a few bucks could easily buy us a fast food lunch. What is it about the pleasure and ease of garbage food that drags me into the gutter of "food like" food? How can I drag my growing daughter in with me? When I am careless about our food she becomes my scapegoat, eating garbage beside me in a thin veil of camaraderie. I seem to have lost my appetite.

On the up side, there is a growing public awareness and desire for better food. The website "100 Days of Real Food" offers a variety of challenges, recipes and forums for people interested in improving their food choices. I have pulled recipes from there, shared posts on Facebook and have even tweeted their messages to my followers. We have begun juicing to increase our intake of the good stuff. I have actually ordered salad or grilled chicken from the drive through. I plan what we are eating at home before we leave the house so I am better prepared against quick, easy and greasy choices.

We keep making better choices and changing our habits. More and more we keep the car on the road and drive past blinking neon signs.

As Sesame Street's Elmo tells my daughter, cookies are a "sometimes food". I have been telling both of us that fast food is a "sometimes food" too. We will leave the garbage for Oscar, OK my Dear?

DEAR MOM

I am (almost) glad that you died when I was thirteen years old. Last night John and I watched the movie "Everybody's Fine" where parenthood and life can go wrong and painful. Afterwards I went up to Libby's bedroom where she was finally asleep, and I lifted her up into my arms, onto my lap and I held her and rocked her and cried into her soft, sweet neck. Then I did the same with Portia. Neither of them woke up, They slept the deep sleep of little girls and good living. I thought of you.

I thought of how you lived, both laughing and sad. How I could understand your drinking better now, you being a single mom back before it was normal. How lonely you must have been despite your friends and family nearby. They weren't at home with us every night. I think about different conversations you and I had, pulling them through the filter of my adulthood. You were the same age when you died as I am right now. You died without us having a last meaningful conversation. You left me rootless and lost despite having a good Dad to live with. At school I was afraid to be left alone in the bathroom, figuring my friends would rush out and leave while I was indisposed.

In spite of this, because of this, I learned to live my love out loud. I took risks. I spoke my mind. I had adventures like moving to Chicago to act instead of spending money and time in college learning about acting. I moved to Denver because I could and I was interested in a scary change. I wanted wilderness of my own with my dog Darby and a blue Honda Civic and a 1,000 mile drive.

I inherited some money from you and could move out of an unhealthy situation and into my very own apartment with your cloth napkins on the table. As I write I realize in flashes it is YOUR table, your tablecloth covered table and cloth napkins that I see just as much as Dad's when I set my table and yearn for family dinners. I can understand more of why good conversation over a meal makes me crazy and controlling. I cannot explain to my three and five year olds that any meal together could be our last before Something Else happens. I cannot both inform them and not scare them, so I swallow the fear and try not to yell when what I imagine and need in my head does not unfold at the dinner table. I try to enjoy the moments for what they are and not what I want them to be.

I have felt the loss of you so many times. I lost the woman in my life who should nurture me through what being woman, mother and wife really means. I've cobbled these life lessons together from other wonderful women in my life instead. I bask in the love from Monte, my mother in law. She loves me well, accepts me in my mess and I am not afraid to be honest with her about most of my struggles. I am grateful for her as my Mother-in-love and I know it is a rare relationship to have.

Sometimes I can speak of you like lines in a play. Other times just seeing a grown woman shopping with her mom brings me to tears so fast I need to turn away. I buy myself things. I buy myself a gift from you instead of for you. I pamper myself on your behalf.

All of this reminds me to make memories for my girls. I feel a lot of pressure from myself to be memorably awesome *just in case* on top of being a mother who disciplines and teaches and guides my girls into strong women. I'm so busy teaching them about the world, life, how not to be greedy, to have good manners, to think of others and to ohmylawdstoptalking that I feel wiped out most days.

But I am also letting them eat Garrett's cheese popcorn in bed in our Chicago hotel. I surprise them with cake for breakfast on their birthdays. We go out for ice-cream in our pajamas. We go on adventures to the craft store and we paint paper plates and boxes and themselves. We cook and bake together making one heck of a mess.

I give my fear of Something Else to God. I beg Him to give us all long, healthy lives. I try to take peace in the lack of control I have. What I can do is love my daughters when they are in front of me. I can teach them through my example and my mistakes. I can love them.

Mom, I will always wonder what we would have been like now. I wonder how you would have lived the rest of your life if there had been more of it. Because you died, I have lived more vibrantly and part of me will always be grateful for your absence. I love you, I miss you, and thank you for your joy and laughter that lives in me. I live my love out loud because of you.

RUNNING MUSIC

I started running several years ago to distract myself from a broken heart and to quit smoking. I hated it. I did about eight 5K races with my Father who has been a three-miles-once-a-week runner for decades. Then I quit. I was happy once again.

In the past few years I married my own Personal Prince Charming and have given birth to our precious first child. Our lives have never been the same. My body is not the same either...so I decided to try running again. In about a month I was able to get up to a slow plodding run interspersed with lots of walking, as usual. I found regular weekly running partners: our baby Portia in a jogging stroller, my Hot Mama friend Tracy on Wednesdays and of course dear old Dad on Monday or Friday.

I have been running longer and better than four years and thirty pounds ago thanks to the maturing process of parenthood, good running partners and my Ipod. The Ipod helps by distracting me from my agony and energizing me with wild happy songs just when I'm ready to give up and eat more french fries. I also have the cool

Nike Plus attachment that tracks all my runs in pretty graphs with stats that keep me motivated to go out one more time. I sometimes miss a run with my Dad or Tracy, but the Ipod is my constant running partner, I won't go out without it. Really.

I was out with my Dad and my Ipod for a longer run and breathlessly mouthing the words to a favorite song in a quiet moment. My Dad said "WHAT?" and I realized what I had sung- "I'm a Barbie Girl, in a Barbie world, I'm plastic, it's fantastic" Funny happy words from a random song on my playlist. I like happy, sexy, songs to keep my tired, sweaty body on task...I am running to be healthier, sure, but above all to be thinner, sexier and to feel good about how I look. It may not be the highest goal in my life, but it is authentic! Later on I was singing about "bringing sexy back" and once again Dad stares at me and comments on the words. This is the man who takes me to Chicago operas, who likes classical music, NPR, and old style country. Pop music is an alien world to him, and as I usually listen to NPR and Christian music, he is surprised at my playlist.

I try to explain to him how the music gets me going and how I know the lyrics are vapid and hardly worth listening to let alone picking up as a daily mantra, but he doesn't understand. He asks, "Do you want your daughter to listen to this junk?" I do have to think about that one. I have already begun reframing my language, both foul and self flagellating, so that when she actually understands words I am giving her the best role model I can summon up. I want her to know she is beautiful, captivating and valuable just as she is, whoever she is. I want her to be confident, kind and love others well.

I know the world may send her a different message. The struggle we women have with body image is an old dragon that never seems to be vanquished. We can know the truth of our beauty in our hearts and then turn on the TV or open a magazine and question our value all over again. We can have thin thighs in college but think they are enormous, not realizing the truth until our thirties when we learn the meaning of ...well, never mind.

Body image can be a real challenge for women and I certainly do not mean to perpetuate it by my running playlist. How do I appreciate the lyrics for what they are without letting them affect me in the negative? How do I protect and shape my daughters' view of herself in a healthy way as she grows into a young woman? Honestly, I don't know. I think that is a process that will take a long time. But I do know that "I'm a Barbie Girl" and Brittany Spear's "Womanizer" help me run faster. They help me run longer. They bring me joy for what they are; silly upbeat dance songs that do not act as a moral guide for my life but keep my feet moving and my sweat pouring and my healthy

beautiful mama's body running. I am happy once
again.

SWEET SPRING SWING

Spring is now here and those fresh, balmy mornings on my tiny front porch have begun. We often eat breakfast on the front porch and dinner on the backyard patio. Being outside is so enjoyable, especially after that endless winter! With these warm Spring days we just drift outside to enjoy the sunshine.

And don't get me started about my hammock! Mother's Day last year was very very good to me. Now we have a lovely hammock that can support 500 pounds of family cuddling! Though I usually kick everybody out and enjoy it all myself. The kids needed something other than my hammock to enjoy in the backyard.

John and I weighed the possibility of a swing set castle treehouse fortress thing. We saw the prices for those suckers and immediately grew nostalgic for a simple metal pole swing set for the girls. They are elusive, it seems. And our yard is the size of a postage stamp. And we live one block from a lovely park anyway. What about...no swing set? Is it un-American to not have a swing set in the yard for our kids? One walk through any subdivision will scream it as part of childhood: You must have your own swing-set-castle-fortress. What if we just...didn't?

My husband had saved a ruined tire from his car a year ago with the thought of a simple tire swing. I thought that might be simply tacky. And dirty. I still struggle with my girls getting dirty. (I know, I know, I am working on it, friends!) A tire swing? A tire swing!

After weighing all of our options and fighting the girls out of my hammock again I began to plot. A tire swing was just what we needed. (Except I'm uncomfortable with heights and do not tie good knots.) John is an Eagle Scout, so tying rope knots would be great if he did it, but if he climbed up a ladder that high he could fall off of it. I asked my Dad to do it. I love him a lot too, but...ummm, let's not say he's dispensable, let's say he has more experience and would be less likely to fall off a ladder to his doom. It sounds better. (Does it sound better?)

The girls and I headed to Home Depot and chatted up a perfectly nice fellow about the merits of this or that rope for a tire swing. I settled on a thick, coarse, natural colored nylon rope but didn't buy it. I was still uncertain about the reality of an old tire hanging in my backyard, so I just took a picture of the rope I wanted with my smartphone.

(Love it!) I listened as my five-year-old daughter Portia quizzed the employee on the different ropes and chains in the aisle. He did his best to answer her questions with respect and a straight face. I thought maybe I should be a little nervous about her fascination, but I was once a little girl in a hardware store. I could remember enjoying the rows of trays of tiny metal things and how different the fragrance of a hardware store was from any other store I would visit.

I also had a tire swing when I was a little girl. I had practically forgotten this fact until my Dad started climbing up the ladder to hang the rope for the swing. We had a large wandering yard and great big walnut trees on our property. I do not know how old I was when the tire swing went up (or who was on it when it broke and came down) but I loved it. I was renewed in my pursuit of a tire swing for the girls. Cheap and now nostalgic: You Bet!

Dad got the swing up and ready without falling to his death from the ladder. We got it the right height. We got it scrubbed clean. I had the girls wash the tire with a bucket of Murphy's Oil Soap and water. I told them it would be white when they cleaned it well enough. When the swing was up we all took turns yahooing around on it and even my Dad had a twirl. GLORIOUS!

My girls may not have the big wooden

activity center of a swing set in their yard, but the park a block away has one. My girls, they have a dirty old tire swing. They push each other on it or clamber onto it together with a few stuffed animals of the day. I watch them as I lounge alone in my hammock almost jealous of their fun and little girl chaos. We all smile and revel under a canopy of leaves in the warm Spring sun.

BLEEP YOU

I may try to look like a lady, but I easily cuss like a sailor. This is not something I am proud of but it is a known fact. The only word I won't use even when I do find situations requiring strong language is the G.D. phrase. Unless I truly want God to damn someone or something, there just isn't any place for that particular combo in my linguistic spiel. It hurts my ears to hear it and it hurts my heart to say it.

So we are clear that bad words do feel fairly at home in my life. Even still, I 'met' someone one weekend who hurt me deeply. I'll call him "Rude T-Shirt Guy". We never spoke, he and I, but I felt so badly for him that I wanted to share the discourse RIGHT NOW even though I meant to be stealing a nap while my cherubs doze.

I was driving happily along doing weekend-y things when I passed a pedestrian male wearing a black t-shirt with large block letters that said "F**** YOU". (There was no asterisk on his shirt however, it was all clearly spelled out for me.) He was a young guy, a bit of a rough looking guy and I thought a lot about him after that.

Who wears that shirt out in public? I'm sure

we all have that kind of day sometimes, but we don't wear it on a t-shirt. What kind of man wants that to be the message that defines him on this particular day? I figure he must be unhappy with his life. I wonder who has hurt him so much and so often that he wants to drive away any other people he may encounter. I guess he must not like himself and has little respect for himself to have so little thought for other people. I felt sad that this man's family might have missed a beat in cherishing him, in supporting him, in loving him out loud every day when he was younger. Was he the kid whose father was abusive instead of loving? Or absent instead of present? Was his brain not as sharp as some other people's causing him to have a rough time in school and get made fun of because of it? Did he just think 'living his rudeness out loud' was funny?

I prayed that this guy would know his special gifts for the world, that someone would value him openly and help heal his hurts. I hope that someone will buy him a better set of t-shirts than the ones I think may be in his dresser drawers.

I also gave thanks for my Dad, family and friends who raised me well with respect for myself and other people. I was grateful to my Mother for caring about others who were less fortunate, who had developmental disabilities or drug problems...because her life taught me to be kinder, to have more empathy for strangers. I was thankful that education was important in my family and among my friends so that I worked to do well and finish college even as an adult.

This Rude T-Shirt Guy made me think of the invisible t-shirts we all wear. What did my t-shirt say today? How do my words, my actions and my face register to other people? Do I really think my sarcasm is helpful? Am I helping someone by judging their looks or behavior against my own? Do I do myself any favors by judging myself against other people who are prettier, thinner, more polished than I think I am? If I am in a hurry and particularly abrupt with a cashier or a friend on the phone...am I living my love out loud at that moment?

Let's wear a shirt every day that says "YOU ARE IMPORTANT!" or maybe "I AM HILARIOUS, WANNA HEAR A JOKE?" or "I WILL SMILE AND INDULGE YOU EVEN THOUGH YOU ARE DRIVING ME NUTS" even "IF THERE ARE ONLY SMALL THINGS I'LL CELEBRATE SOMETHING TODAY!" What if Rude T-Shirt Guy's big block letters simply read "THANK YOU"? How would that have changed his day, let alone mine?

What do you hope your t-shirt said to the people who read it today? What do you think it actually said? Whatever will you wear tomorrow?

COMPLAINT DEPARTMENT

Sometimes I think I am pretty important. I spend my days with two Tiny Girls who think THEY are pretty important. At times this causes a bit of a conflict and I'm not sure who whines the loudest about it. If you want to see just how messed up you are and how out of control of life you can be, have a few kids. Every flaw is exposed as you try to raise them to be good folks: "Don't talk with your mouth full" quickly proved to me that I myself need to be taught this lesson. FAST. Do you know how hard it is to tell your toddler not to talk with their mouth full when your mouth is in fact full of food??? Selfish power struggles with a toddler while an infant cries can drive the strongest Mama straight into the potato chip bag headfirst. Stay at home mamas don't get overweight from having children, it is from trying to raise their children!

I have struggled to maintain the peace and raise my girls well, but the stress of my days often means by the end of each one I am not the sweetest woman to be around. I often hurl the myriad challenges of my day at my husband as soon as he walks through the door. Sometimes dinner isn't made and the house looks like a toy bomb went off and I feel guilty about it. When I try to explain how the day went down I think it is a lot more like complaining than anything helpful.

I started reading a fabulous book by Gretchen Rubin called "The Happiness Project". In it she accounts for all the sources of happiness available to us and she attempts to try her version of them during her year long project. The book and her blog have been helpful to me. I am trying to find new sources of happiness and pleasure as my life changes via having children. Gone are cocktails out on the town(I can barely finish a glass of wine nowadays!), hello collapsing on the couch in front of the boob tube after kids are in bed. There has to be more to my life and complaining about it is not improving the situation.

A recent church service I attended had one point I have carried with me through the week; Meet others needs even when mine aren't met. Our natural inclination is to under-serve others if our needs aren't met. To not bother helping someone else when we are so tired, worn out and used up from daily life. Instead, we should look to serve someone who needs a little help. This will get the focus off of ourselves and onto the good we create for someone else. I really like this idea and it has helped me many times to gain a healthier perspective on my current tiny woes.

This is not to say we don't need to take care of ourselves. We do. But maybe instead of focusing on where our life is lacking, instead of complaining about all the little deaths within our days, we can fill ourselves up by serving someone else. Complaining is an energy drain for both the complainer and the complainee. The satisfaction from doing it is short lived and nothing ever changes because of it.

If you hear me (or yourself) whining beyond what is tolerable, do as my husband did just this morning: put us in a time out until we have a change of attitude. Sitting on the hall bench next to my daughter's timeout chair is a fast reminder that while my needs are important, my Complaint Department needs to be closed. Is your Complaint Department open? To complain simply proves how ungrateful I am. This is not what I want to teach my girls, or how I want to live my daily life. How about you?

POLE AEROBICS
MADE ME FAT

My awesome "Mothers and More" group hosted this month's mingle at a dance class. To be more specific, a pole dancing class. We are all mamas and usually of young kidlets so any attempt to "bring sexy back" is either welcome or a subtle annoyance getting between us and more sleep! So Pole Dancing Class. RIGHT. Well, they called it Pole Aerobics but you all get the idea, yes?

I think I used to be a sexy woman, so my 40 year old thirty-pounds-overweight loose-neck-skin mama self decided to go. I put on makeup and did my hair. For an exercise class. I thought them calling it an exercise class was a *wink wink nod nod* to encourage more women to attend but they were serious. I was the only one in a sparkly tank top and lacy bra, I will tell ya that.

The instructor was a woman so appropriately named "Summer". I think she was pretty young. Like twelve. She was at least a real woman in the figure department....pretty curvy and strong like bull. I was so excited to take this class. THEN, I was more excited *to get out of* this class. Pole aerobics class made me fatter!!

I am not just a little fat (although clothes can hide it) I am also so very weak. How about no core strength at all? My favorite yoga instructor Kim Sellers talks about using our core strength all the time. One of the moves involved holding onto the pole and lifting up both legs, sexy style, but most of us were laughing and flailing about in a decidedly unsexy manner. Parenting magazines talk about how defined my arm muscles must be from hefting thirty-pound toddlers all day. Well. My arms must have missed the memo. How about floppy arms where apparently the muscles have fallen from the bicep area down into the tricep area and just hang there. Doing Nothing. I couldn't pull myself up the pole for anything. It was probably sad to see.

I didn't realize how bad off I truly was until taking this little class.

I knew I should have had a drink or two (or six) beforehand. Only one of our number was able to follow Summer in all parts of the routine. The routine in which one backs up to the pole, somehow wraps her legs around it, pushes up said pole with legs and arms, then slides all the way down to the floor and crawls forward. Sexily. Riiiiight. Um, usually the biggest trick I can pull off is taking a shower. Maybe I will strike a match to light a candle. The only crawling on the floor this mama does is to find lost toys under the couch. Well.

But here is the silver (matches my tank top) lining: I am more motivated. I want STRENGTH. I want arms that can do something. I want a core that lets me pull something up from somewhere else instead of laughing, standing there, unable to lift a single thing. I took this pole dancing class. because I wanted to feel sexy, instead I got an ugly wake up call. And I answered. Core and arms: My priority!

Summer, we probably won't see each other again. EVER. But you taught me more than you could know, thank you, thank you thank you! Now, I guess I should start with some pushups. Yuck.

OK, here we go!

Friend, you count 'em.

BICYCLE OBSESSED

They say less is more, but I'm a girl for whom more is more. I like things a lot. I am zealous and easily obsessed or excitable. I live my life well most days, but my obsessions can make me a little crazy. I guess I am a binger. I'm a little bingey. I bingeth. I am a woman bingeonified. Of course that was a word before I used it.

One of my latest obsessions has been cargo bikes. I've been biking more for daily errands and thus carrying more of whatever else I might be obsessed with upon my bicycle. My little girls are squished together in the trailer on trips to school drop off. My front basket gets loaded down with whatever we find at the farmer's market to eat. I want to do even more with my bicycle. I want to pretend I am brave enough to sell our second car and do without. A cargo bike could make that more realistic. I have eaten, slept and dreamed about cargo bikes the past six months. A longtail? A box bike? Madsen? Yuba? Xtracycle? I've pinned them on Pinterest. I've liked them on Facebook. I've test ridden them, borrowed them, drooled over them.

Alongside my new cargo bike obsession I am getting an education on bicycling in general.

I've devoured two books by Elly Blue; Bikenomics and Everyday Bicycling. I bought an extra copy so if you want to borrow it, let me know! I'm getting more active as a voice of the mama who wants to bicycle more (and more safely) with her kids. I'm joining local and national bicycling groups online like League of American Cyclists to learn more about bike advocacy and bike safety.

One of the surprises I've discovered in my everyday riding is the valuable bicycle conversations with strangers. They like the music I play from the handlebars--compliments of a cell phone mount and Pandora. I often listen to Squirrel Nut Zippers or Squeeze just for sass. I've had friends ask, "Do you really ride your bike to Target?" Yes I do, I tell them. I get to encourage them to ride more, to ride farther. Like me, they realize it is only a mindset that they can only drive the car 'there'.

There is some planning involved in biking as transportation. When I first biked to a place I'd only driven before, it was an adventure. As a stay at home mama I don't get a lot of adventure outside of scraped knees and mystery food in our refrigerator. Embarking on my bike to the grocery store was exciting. It was a little scary. What if I got a flat tire? What if I got hit by a car? But then again, riding in the car is risky too. I also believe I am a better driver on a bicycle than in a car. I do not take my safety for granted . I am observant and vigilant and I pray a lot.

My worries are shallower too: What if I bought too much and couldn't get it home on the bicycle? This alone keeps me from shopping like I might do otherwise. I discovered I buy less because I am biking more. I am also saving money to buy a better, bigger bike. A cargo bike? Or at least a Bobike child's seat for my older daughter. She's 5 years old now and the Bobike Junior is for kids up to ten years old! It will be a safer alternative to Portia riding on my rear rack, which we call our fake cargo bike. We had an accident with her precious foot and the spokes and I saw the value of spending money to ride safer. I'm remorseful and embarrassed we needed a scary accident to get me ready to spend money on quality equipment. We continue to bike and are not scared off from biking despite our mishaps.

And then this week I drove to the gym at four-thirty a.m. because I was afraid I would not have the energy after class to bike home again. There was an NPR piece on global warming and how birds are in danger of becoming extinct. I felt the weight of my own responsibility to our environment. I felt embarrassed and foolish to be so blessed that I could drive to the gym to get exercise. I can do something to reduce global warming by biking instead of driving even once a week. I vowed to bike to the gym next time, even at four-thirty a.m. It is only three miles from home

and I like birds a lot. Almost as much as I like...
love...biking.

HUMBLED
HANDLESS

Yesterday at a church we were visiting I was people watching instead of praying. As we sang songs and started up the worship service I was admiring a young mother with a new baby. The woman was beautiful and had a cute t-shirt and green skirt on, her young husband standing happily beside her. Their newborn baby was hard to see as he was tucked safely in his carrier on the floor but I kept looking. From my vantage point he had beautiful pale cocoa colored skin, a lovely mix of his black mother and his white father. I loved this little family and wished I knew them.

As a new mom myself I am particularly fascinated by every baby I can lay my eyes on and I love chatting up the parents. I just kept watching this family until I noticed the woman's arm; there was no hand on it! I was stunned, my stomach hurt for her and my mind raced about all the daily tasks of caring for a baby...how could she possibly manage any of it? I kept staring ardently, searching for a glimpse of her other arm. I was desperate to know there was a beautiful fully functioning hand on the other arm at least. There was not. Tears filled my eyes and I told my husband I was going for a drink of water as I quickly left my seat.

I went to the ladies room to compose myself and to pray a blessing on the family. I also spent time reacquainting myself with the abundance of blessings in my life I am already aware of and also those I take for granted. Like having hands. My heart hurts even now for them. The day before I had had what I thought was a bad day--nothing really went my way, the baby was teething so all of us were tired and cranky. I know everything important like food, shelter and clothing is more than taken care of, we are quite comfortable. I have an excellent husband who loves me well and helps out doing more than his fair share around the house. Even knowing this, it still felt like a bad day and I chose to be in a foul mood through most of it. How differently I may have lived if Sunday came before Saturday this week.

How do you put on or take off a diaper without fingers, with no hands? How do you put a pacifier in a tiny baby mouth, how do you breastfeed or fix a bottle without hands? I asked a dear friend from the church about the woman and if she knew her. She said they were visiting someone there and that the girl was a Rwandan refugee. She had probably lost her hands as a young child. I realize she is probably used to functioning without hands, but I'm not used to it. I was sick with the thought of how many children and adults this had happened to. I was embarrassed with my lack of deep interest in some world events that do not touch me directly. I was disappointed in the kind of person I had been the day before.

I wanted to go to the young mother, to hug her and tell her...what? "Gosh, I'm glad I'm not you and I sure learned a lesson today?" or "God blessed me with you today, I sure hope I remember this lesson later in my life- or later in the week even when I feel sorry for my spoiled little self?" How could I say that? How could I tell her she was more beautiful to me in the story her body now told? How could I ask all of my questions about caring for a baby without having any hands? How can I stop thinking of how lucky I am to get up in the middle of the night- twice- to hold my crying baby girl and rock her back to sleep? I cannot.

Instead of stumbling for a way to bless her directly, I will tell this story to you, in the hopes you will remember it when you are feeling sorry for yourself about something. Remember this young mother and her precious family and if you can, say a prayer that she has all the hands she needs to live a beautiful life.

NEKKID YOGA CHALLENGE

Once Upon A Time, when I was fat in the way only a healthy twenty-five year old girl can be fat (i.e.: perfect with tiny flaws only she can see with the help of three hand mirrors and a bad romance) I did yoga naked. Well mostly naked. In the secluded backyard of my friend's house, with two wonderful gal pals, we did (almost) naked yoga one fine summer day. It was glorious: warm sun shining on our nubile bodies, wind rustling our hair. The naughtiness of it was thrilling and dangerous...until we heard someone call out! You should have seen how fast we moved when we saw the surprise male visitor coming up the driveway! We made his day.

Later I practiced "brag" yoga in front of my husband when we were dating. (See how sexy and flexible I am? You better put a ring on it!) I pictured myself as strong. I saw myself doing yoga as sexy, even in yoga pants.

Seven years later and I rarely do yoga in front of him. I certainly do not do it naked. When I was younger and lived alone, I had naked time all the time. I used to languish about all afternoon, munching grapes and reading on my couch, naked. I was comfortable in my skin. I valued myself and I felt lovely. Things are different now. As I have aged and grown fatter as a forty-two year old mother of two, I struggle with my mama body. I work harder to feel beautiful and it involves more makeup, more hair products. More clothing layers.

Then I read a Huffington Post blog on moms and their swimsuits. The author Jessica Turner's words keep rattling around in my brain, speaking beauty and acceptance into my womanly soul. I cannot wait to flaunt my abundant posterior at the next beach day. I won't hide on my beach blanket any more. I will PLAY. Thank you, Jessica Turner, for reminding me about what matters.

I kept thinking about Turner's beautiful words and realized I have grown apologetic about my body. I self-consciously hide it. I dim the lights at night. I wear pajamas and dressing gowns. I add layers even in the summer heat. I still do yoga, but it is less of a celebration of my body and more of a maintenance plan.

Today I did yoga naked in front of my husband and in front of my daughters. I had something to discover about myself. I needed to rise to the challenge and woke up inspired. I took my lovely naked self downstairs and did fifteen minutes of YogaGlo yoga. Naked. I felt vulnerable, anxious, and proud of myself. I felt accepting of my body. It was wonderful. It was embarrassing. It was almost as good as the outdoor naked yoga, but I do not have enough privacy fence to make that happen. Ever again. But today was great.

When she woke up and came downstairs, my little daughter only asked me two questions, "Mama, why are you naked?"

I told her I wanted to be thankful for what God gave me, even if it's shifted. I told her I wanted to have a little naked time and do my yoga this morning. She took that in stride. Any kid can understand their Mama wanting "Naked Saturday" on a Tuesday morning instead.

Then she asked the best question ever, "why aren't they naked?" as she pointed to the on screen instructor. I stifled a chortle and smiled, "because that is another kind of channel entirely, My Love!"

SEASONAL TRUTH

Now that Christmas is over, I'm thinking of some seasonal truths I want to take with me into the New Year. There are (of course) some standard old saws about over indulgence, and children liking the boxes presents came in as much as the gifts and how to keep Christmas all year long, in your heart. I'm not there this year, friends! After feeling smug about our healthy family for the past years, kindergarten hit and it has been plague after plague of infectious ills. We have been too busy with too much fun and I'm tired. Although I have enjoyed Christmas mightily, the following seasonal truths will carry me through the process of un-Christmasing our home this year.

1)   If I didn't get a Christmas card out by Christmas Day, I should stop telling myself I'll do a New Year's Card instead. Not happening. Only one person sends out a New Year's Card and I am lucky enough just to receive theirs.

2)   If an ornament or other holiday doodah is "kinda" broken, I should do it the honor of properly disposing of it. Every time I see it I'm sad it is experiencing demise, feel guilty I didn't wrap it in bubble wrap all these years, and think up ways

to repair or salvage it next year that I will never follow through with. I need to put us both out of our misery and chuck it. Ditto "kinda" working light strings. Chuck 'em!

3)   I am training my kids to be consumers or stewards of the world around them. If I would rather they become stewards, I should engage and involve them in the "one in one out" policy for new toys. For each item they unwrapped for Christmas, they should find another item to donate. I'll make it easy and get them a box to fill up.

4)   Volunteering fills my heart up any time of year, but it is easiest to do it at Christmas time. Why is that? If I want to experience the immediate education that serving others brings me, I need to plan to do that monthly instead of just during the holidays. EVERYONE benefits from serving ANYONE in a volunteer capacity. The quickest way to appreciate my little house and life is not to improve upon it, but to improve someone else's life, even just a little tiny bit.

5)   Holiday Hangovers Happen. Too much joy, too much food, too many parties and celebratory moments leave most of us feeling a little blue. Sure, we've got New Year's, but if you have little bitty kids, well you don't really have New Year's anymore, do you? To help with my holiday hangover, I think I will make a plan to fully engage with the world this next year. I'll exercise

more....every day! I'll eat less junk and more fruits and veggies...I'll cuss less. I'll follow #4 and volunteer monthly(...what?...oh... I guess these do sound like New Years Resolutions. Umm....)

New Year's Resolutions serve a purpose but are rarely followed to the satisfaction of the individual. We like newness and we like the idea of change. In making New Year's resolutions we solve number five, the Christmas Hangover, we plan to be better people this next year by number four: volunteering! We find ways to express our desire to (number three) be better people, better stewards of our lives and families, we vow to be more proactive, say by (number two) chucking those bloody Christmas string lights that barely work and we plan to (number one) simplify our lives by removing the clutter of things that no longer delight or better us as people!

Maybe all I need to do after Christmas is start my New Year's Resolutions! Maybe then I won't feel such a longing for more Christmas carols, some actual snow, and one more present I wanted but didn't get. Maybe these seasonal truths should be set aside until next year. I'm going to go work on my New Year's Resolutions. After I pack up a few more decorations...I can probably repair this one next year. *yawn* Or maybe...just a post Christmas nap?

SING FOR YOUR SUPPER

I want to hang out with some adults and have a conversation not punctuated with "No more TV!" or "WAITAMINUTE....What are those markers, tape and stapler for?!?" Charades and Card Games are a snooze. I'm not quite ready for Bingo Hall yet. I have little kids, so how exactly could I throw an elegant dinner party? (Oh yeah, and on a budget!) And without much effort. I did it as a single woman, and I did it as a married mama to two little crazy monkeys: Invite your friends to a "Sing for Your Supper" dinner party!

Back before TV and the Interweb there was such a thing as conversation. It was practically an art form. Evenings were also filled with someone playing a piano and others joining in. A guest may tell a colorful story or perform if they have some unique skill. I doubt this happens in most homes today and it rarely happens in mine. We do use cloth napkins and I probably light some candles once or twice a week but that is it. We are missing something, friends!

On the Daily Connoisseur blog Jennifer

Stevens talks about the French way of preparing a big dinner with several leisurely courses, conversation and connectedness. Most every night. They listened to classical music. Candles were lit. Feeding wasn't a paper wrapped and styrofoam box event...it was elegant. I think our souls could use more of this. Unless your soul is cringing. If your soul cringes, simply stop listening to this and go do something that makes you feel awesome, I won't be offended, I promise. (Run along. Go ahead, it is ok.)

OK. For the rest of you. Use evite or email or just pick up the phone. The more elegant and fancy you make it the more work you have to do, so whatever works for you. Maybe you prepare the whole meal, maybe you invite folks to bring potluck. I've done both. Invite people to dress down or up, although I must say the latter is usually more festive. The key to a Sing for Your Supper dinner is you invite your guests to prepare something to present. It can be a poem they read or recite from memory. It can be a song sung or played. It can be a joke or series of jokes. I had a few poetry and joke books available so if someone wasn't prepared but wanted to be involved once the fun started they could easily step into the fray.

There is a fun game for anyone who doesn't perform: "How Many Marshmallows Can You Stuff Into Your Mouth?" Hilarious audience participation too, as we needed to count for each contender. Keep napkins handy.

Usually the performances come at the end of dinner and before dessert, but again it is YOUR party. Do exactly what pleases you. Candlelight and classical music cast the spell of a bygone era and I highly recommend them. (Even if dinner, served on china plates, mais bien sur, came from paper or styrofoam containers!) And I would love to hear about your party afterwards. (Especially if you have video or photos!) Bon Appetit!

EXERCISE IS MY TANTRUM

We all have stress that makes us want to run screaming from the place we are in towards anything simpler and less...stressful. If you have short people in your life and spend lots of time around them you probably want to get down on the floor with them some days and have your own tantrum thank you very much. In your work life when you are so hemmed in by red tape and policy or so frustrated with people who aren't as (brilliant) broad minded as you are, a little floor rolling hollering tantrum might be just the thing.

We all want Our Way no matter what direction that may take our lives. Stress is pretty common in a world where lots of very different individuals want Their Way. After our second babe was born instead of it being My Way or the Highway, My Way literally hit the highway and our world has been run to some extent by folks who are not even two feet tall. FRUSTRATING. Difficult. Maddening. Stressful.

I talked to friends about parenting trials and sought advice. My friend Carrie had one word for me: "Kickboxing." I wasn't too thrilled, the word I was hoping for was "Cupcakes" or "Alcohol". I went to the doctor to get input on my stress induced funk and she suggested exercise too. These people obviously didn't understand how relaxing and de-stressing for me usually included my ample posterior on a soft surface and a cold adult bevvie in my hand. (OK...also a bowl of something sweet or salty or both in my lap). Just the thought of exercising gave me more stress. Even so, I decided I had to do something different. So I started walking with the baby girls in the jogging stroller. Then I started walking a bit faster, lo, even breaking a sweat! The Husband and I decided to take on a Couch to 5K training group as a tribute to our fourth wedding anniversary theme which was "wood". The final 5K run was a trail run through...wait for it, YUP! The woods. As we went week after week walking less and running more (and faster too!) I noticed that every good day I had began with a run.

On the advice of my doctor and my friend Carrie I was taking frustration out on the pavement instead of my kids (which is never a good way to parent anyway). Any sense of laziness, disappointment, anger, sadness or frustration was smaller when I returned home from running. Because I took care of myself first thing in the morning by exercising, I had more energy to take care of these two tiny girls I love most in the world. I had essentially begun making exercise my tantrum.

Instead of yelling I was wheezing. Instead of flailing on the floor I was flailing through neighborhoods. Instead of losing control of myself I was gaining it and decided that exercise would be a most days event for a long while. Not to get thinner. Not to be healthier. Exercise would free me from the heavy stress of loving people with a different worldview than mine. Exercise would help me to take better care of other people because I was taking care of myself. Exercise as my tantrum began turning a negative around to a positive energy and that makes me keep going with a big sweaty smile on my face. Most Days at least.

VOTE LOCAL

How 'bout those Presidential Candidate Debates? People are excited or scared or mortified by the candidates and the muckraking of a national election. They watch debates, Facebook about their favorite candidates, and talk with friends. These same people may not even be aware of their city's local elections (the national election's forlorn stepchild). I rarely voted in local elections before getting married to John who loves politics. I would vote only for presidents and when I voted it was usually a straight ticket. I was raised to care about elections, I just didn't. I got a kick out of my Grandmother Lutes' joke that she was a Democrat and Grandpa Willard was a Republican (or vice versa?) and so when they voted they canceled each other out. I thought, "Why bother?" I was raised to care about elections, I just didn't.

After getting married, I usually asked my husband John what he thought of political candidates because I knew he was smart and paid attention. And he cared. I began voting in local elections because I was apparently a grown up and it was the thing to do. I read apathetically about pending candidates and voted. I voted. And I voted.

Now after going door to door to get John on the Valparaiso, Indiana city council ballot, after campaigning beside him, meeting other candidates, going to the forum and actually READING the newspaper articles about the upcoming election: I care. I know how foolish a person sounds who says "Ohhh...I don't vote". I want to ask if they have other people make all of their other decisions for them. I realize that in not being aware and informed, in not caring much for politics, I let other people speak for me and they rarely get it right.

I now realize my apathy makes me, my parents and family look ignorant, as if they hadn't coached, prodded and cajoled me to care about my own civic engagement. After this campaign I realize how hard a candidate can work just to get their name on a piece of paper. And then again how much work and money can go into asking enough people to notice their name, to read that name and to mark the box next to the name. I know how important it is because I have done the work. I have called voters, asking them to check the box next to my husband's name. I know what I think of the person who says, "Oh, I don't bother voting in local elections."

This man I married doesn't want fame; he is an introvert. He doesn't care about popularity.

He got a taste of public service in college and grad school and he liked the deep work, thought and honor of it. I love this about him even though I did not share his passion when we began. After our adventure, after casting our ballot during early voting together one quiet weekday afternoon, after all the friends and family and neighbors handing him their money or their time or their encouragement, I share his respect for politics. I am interested. I am no longer apathetic.

I talked today with a group about the change in me. I said I thought if people who do not care about elections worked even a tiny bit on any campaign they might see it differently. Please consider volunteering on a committee or helping a local or national candidate at the local level. We feel so removed from politics that we think it doesn't matter anyway. It does. It matters.

My husband recently wrote,

"There have been a number of people I have spoken to over the last couple of years who express being disenfranchised by the local political process. They feel their vote and their voice doesn't count. Indeed in 2007 voter turnout in Porter County for local elections was 32%. In the last local election in 2011, the voter turnout dropped to 25% in the county. That kind of voter apathy could signal a type of learned helplessness that people feel when they have no say in our local representative democracy. In fact, local elections probably have a larger impact on the voting public than any state or national election."

John inspired me not just by his words but by his actions. He put his passion into action and put his desire to work and it affected both of us. Even our four and six year old daughters have stump speeches ready for their father. I even considered collecting signatures at the polls back in November to get Bernie on the ballot for President. decided to take this one election at a time.

John wanted to run for office to serve his city, his neighbors, and to make a difference in all of our lives. I hope he knows the difference he has made in my life. Please vote wherever you are, for whoever you believe in, every chance you get in every election. It makes a difference. You can make the difference. Your vote counts. My vote counts too.

FOLDING FRENZY

I can understand why my parents were so boring when I was a kid: They were tired. They were not adventurous, or wild or fun or carefree. They were careful and worried and tired and it was my fault. MY FAULT! I've heard people say that having children greatly decreases your happiness but somehow increases your joy. For me children, marriage and domesticity have just made me crazy. It is delightful.

I used to talk about sex. I used to think about it. Now as I've aged and have this deeply engaged marriage of eight years and fairly manageable parenthood thing going on, I've slid into being the tired and uptight Mother instead of a wild and free Bombshell. It would almost be scary if it weren't so satisfying. This must be a sign I have actually lost my mind.

Allow me to clarify the happy tragedy that is my descent into middle age: FOLDING. If you have paid attention I have complained endlessly about laundry. First World problems, forgive me, but still I struggle. I must have equated laundry with full on domestication and bucked the bit and saddle there until just recently. I like to read self help books on organizing and then lose them in a random unorganized pile somewhere. Are you with me?

Then I heard about this book "The Magic Art of Tidying Up" by Japanese author Marie Kondo. I heard the author was cuckoo. I heard she was brilliant. Eventually I bought the E book and even though I only read half of it, it has changed my view of life and laundry. The book has helped me settle into domestic middle age with contentment. It started with a video and ended in a sock drawer.

This crazy author has become so popular with middle aged housewives looking for a clear path to domestic insanity that something like a billion bloggers have posted about the book. I saw a video on folding the "KonMari" way as the author calls it. The video amused me in its attention to detail. I am a crummy folder. If I even get to folding. Our nanny Hannah this summer was so helpful and folded most of our duds all summer. And she folded like she had worked at the Gap. I asked her how she learned to fold so well and she looked at me askance as if she could tell my mind was going fast. Her mother is obviously just awesome to have raised her to fold clothes so well.

I kept thinking of the video and finally one morning I woke up wanting to try to fold differently. I did it . OH! MY! My eyes lingered on the folded shirts stacked on edge; it was easy to see what was there and I felt the satisfaction of doing a job well. I resisted redoing all my other drawers right then. Later I was laying out some clothes for John for our family vacation and I stared at his shirts in the drawer. I kinda wanted to refold them. (The right way.) I knew it was crazy to not only want to fold, but to be willing to refold perfectly good and already folded clothes. I told you I was crazy, what do you think I did?

Then I moved on to socks. As I read Marie's thoughts on socks she said they work hard and need to rest. Did you know your socks need rest? Me neither. She said when they are balled up or knotted they cannot rest and they should be neatly folded and stacked on edge (like ties in a department store). I rolled my eyes, but couldn't help peering into my sock drawer. It still embarrasses me to say it, but I saw my socks and they needed a drink! They were stressed and forlorn. I laughed at myself as I began to unfurl them and smooth them into tidy folds. When I finished the drawer was so relaxing to look at I actually showed it off to several people who now suddenly won't return my calls. But my socks look great.

I love the sense of well being I get from actually doing the laundry instead of fretting about it. It might be sad to be more interested in folding on top of the washing machine instead of...but it is what it is. And actually, having this euphoric sense of accomplishment from an unremarkable chore improves my mood and makes me feel better in other areas of my life. As a matter of fact, I might park the kids in front of the TV for a bit and show my husband the other magic benefits of a folded sock drawer.

WATER WAYS

As I wrote my short section of the Michiana Chronicles honoring South Bend's 150th Birthday, the love story between downtown, its waterways and my heart revealed itself as follows:

This city of ours taught me some things one might not expect: to seek adventure, to appreciate a sense of wonder and expect excitement in architecture. South Bend showed me how the history and life of a place imprints itself into your bones.

When I was eight years old my parents got a divorce, which meant my Dad only saw me on Wednesday nights for dinner and every other weekend. On his weekends we often headed to downtown South Bend, to the Century Center and what is now known as the Island Park Pavilion.

We would sit on the wide cement wall overlooking the Fire Catcher statue I never appreciated and the waterfalls. As we ate a picnic lunch the heavy rush of that water would transfix me. I was breathless with the mix of fear and awe and excitement only a little dangerous beauty can bring.

We would finish eating and wander the lower paths beside the river, onto floating docks that may still be there. We would wander the various picnic areas and benches, talking and exploring. It felt like we were in a different country. This time with my Father along the water and structures of downtown South Bend and the St. Joseph River primed my eye for interesting sights. It taught me from childhood to expect more from my surroundings and to appreciate adventure.

On special occasions we would eat fancy brunch with cloth napkins at the Marriott hotel. I can still taste what four helpings of chocolate mousse in glass parfait cups was like: Heaven. After brunch we would wander under the soaring glass ceilinged atrium and out to the various paths around the river. We would wander near Century Center, the island and waterfall and floating docks but this time, in dress up clothes!

I grew up mostly in South Bend but as a young adult I left to explore city life in Chicago and then mountains in Colorado. But I came back. I came back to "The Bend" again because it was always home. I came back to buy a house on Altgeld Street and live a happy life on the South Side near where I was born.

As an adult I walked and ran with friends along the newer sections of the East Race

Waterway. Its sprawling paths once again brought me to the waterfalls, Century Center, now also Seitz Park, the Firefighter's Statue. We would pause to stare into the rushing waterfalls and the East Race's churning white water. I was thrilled at the macabre thought of what it might feel like to plunge into the cold rushing water. I admired its beauty with awe and a little fear. I remembered my childhood adventures with bittersweet fondness.

One time I wandered from South Bend Chocolate Cafe with a first date and we crossed through the paths by Century Center and ventured to the firefighter's memorial statue to hunt for a geocache. We found it in a plastic film canister, under a bench with a great view of Century Center, the Firecatcher. It was romantic but we didn't hold hands or anything; It was a first date after all! He and I talked and walked and marveled at the rushing water like so many romantic couples do along the St. Joe River paths.

Less than one year later, that first date fellow, John Novak, would propose to me on that very site. Right after I gazed across the water to the Century Center and the rushing waterfall and the Firecatcher statue I still didn't admire. I think I was even telling him about those childhood thoughts and wanderings when I turned around to see his face. I actually stopped talking for a moment. He proposed with a diamond ring in a geocache film canister. Photographer Cathy Dietz got it on camera and we were married in the glass atrium of the Marriott Hotel under those soaring glass walls and windows of my childhood.

Later still I pushed my daughters in strollers along the paths near Century Center, to and from the Farmer's Market. I showed them the high glass atrium where I married their father and the waterfalls surrounding the paths. From my childhood to theirs... As I write this I think it has been too long since my daughters and I walked along the river and the waterways downtown. Maybe I will ask them what they see in that large modern art statue. I will hold hands this time with that First Date Fellow. We can invite my Dad along too, to remind me through my daughters of the ways of water through a young girl's heart.

NEW YEAR'S REVOLUTION

When I realized I would be chatting with you fine WVPE listeners on New Year's Day, I wondered what fresh insight I could offer. I am not clever enough to reintroduce New Year's Resolutions. I have never been close to successful in accomplishing even one of mine. Ever. I figured to truly have a fresh thought for this fresh new year of 2016, I had to start anew. I had to ask someone younger. Much younger, like six. (six and a half!) My daughter Portia agreed to help and this is what happened.

I asked what she thought about a whole fresh new year starting. She said "It sounds wonderful!" Then I asked, Portia, what are your New Year's Resolutions for 2016? She leaned in and said, "What are revolutions?" I explained that New Year's resolutions are a standard custom for people around us to choose some things we want to do better and list them to focus on improving in the next year. Portia said she thought that sounded like a good idea.

Now I have tried and failed like most of

you to accomplish resolutions, some of which have been :

1. Stop Swearing.

2. Stop eating all the food all the time.

3. Exercise more often than once in a while. (Sometimes I fantasize about actually being "FIT". And it all ends there, folks.)

Here is a spoiler alert: I'm forty-uh-<u>thirty</u> something(30 plus fourteen but who's counting?) and still cussing, still hungry, still grouchy, I still leave dirty dishes in the sink too long and still overweight. HAPPY NEW YEAR!

I figured Portia might have better ideas for New Year's Resolutions than I did. So I asked her what three things she would like to personally improve upon in 2016. Here is what she said:

1. I want to be a good artist.

2. This year, my birthday, I really want to prove it can be a ninja birthday.

3. That I am really good in school.

Then I asked Portia what she thought my top three New Year's Resolutions for 2016 should be, and she said;

1. "Being a better mommy: teaching me and Libby, my younger sister, how to be a better mom when

we grow up. (I asked how I would do that and she said that I should do my best at being a great mama by showing them how to behave.")

2. "You could teach me how to be a better artist and be better at art by practicing the rest of this year in your new mama coloring book you got for Christmas."

3. "You could try being better at baking because you just need practice because I think you can practice and practice over and over again and be a professional like Grace the American Girl Doll that I have that was Girl of the Year in 2015. "

Okay, those seem doable except for all the baking. There is no way we are opening a French bakery like her doll in the books. I'd be happy to eat at a French bakery, but this ends there. I thought a younger approach could be accidentally insightful, but at the end of the day I just do not know.

I love the fresh new start of the New Year and I actually love writing down resolutions in my journal using my best handwriting. I just cannot follow through with them. This has happened long enough I am about to give up. Or change things. What did Portia call them, Revolutions? Vive la Revolution! What if instead of changing a few ugly habits I say "No thanks" and have an annual Revolution, New Year's Revolution: I resolve to not resolve. I resolve to have a revolution in my life where I just take each day as it comes.

I do not plan to be any better thinner, smarter or tidier than I already am.

Instead of pretending I might strive this year, I can just choose to enjoy exactly who I am and what is in front of me. I don't think it would be settling really; rather it is an upheaval of my old ways and a marvelous sort of New Year's "Revolution" we could all get behind. So rip that blankety-blank list up, pass the Cheetos and let's skip the gym to sleep in: Happy New Year my friends!

DREAMING OF OTHER SEASONS

"I'm melting! I'm melting!" If you listened carefully, did you hear that this week coming from our streets and sidewalks and yards? The nasty stuff was everywhere. White or brown, or even worse: yellow. I'm glad to see it go, even just for now. The piles.

I'm good with the seasons, one of the things I love about living in northern Indiana: Seasons. About the time I am sick of the cold, along comes that fresh breath of Spring with its hopeful sunshine. My little girls and I eat our breakfast on our tiny front porch every chance we get as it warms. Still in our pjs, covered with blankets against the chill in the air, we dine alfresco! After breakfast, we wander around the front or back yard in our wellies. We admire the mud, we try to decide if the green shoots are weeds or some kind of lovely plant. We decide it is most likely weeds. We leave the poor thing alone and wander on. We may consider doing a bit of yard work as we wander but most likely we won't. Our mornings are lazy and it is difficult to pull weeds or tidy a yard with a coffee cup in hand.

Soon it becomes warmer, even hot and I love basking in the sunshine. Once again, we are breakfasting on the tiny porch. When the three of us are sitting, there is barely enough room to let the dog inside (or outside for that matter). Tiny. Porch. I have too much furniture for the 20 square foot space: A vintage battleship of a glider and a few chairs including a child's rocker we rescued from a neighbor's trash pile.

We spend our early summer mornings out there on the tiny porch but then hurry inside to the cool air-conditioning. Occasionally we wander through the yard and admire the weeds and surprise flowers. If I've stashed the gardening gloves and a trowel on the porch, I may pull a few weeds. Most likely I will wander about with my coffee cup, looking at but not tending that garden. Those weeds.

Sometimes we go to spend our day at Lake Michigan where it is cooler. Other days we sit in our little backyard on the patio. The girls play in the yard and I can watch them falling out of the hammock. Sweat pools in places I'd rather not mention.

Just as I am so very tired of sweating and sand everywhere even if we haven't gone to the lake yet that week...the air cools and shifts and it smells businesslike. Shuffling through the brown and gold leaves on the sidewalk makes a scraping, shushing sound that's deafening. The start of school and darkening of days reminds all of us to get serious. We spend fewer mornings on the tiny porch. Instead there is oatmeal for breakfast, too sloppy to eat in our laps and so we are inside, at the dinner table. If I walk through the yard or garden it is to go somewhere else. Maybe I will refill a bird feeder. I'll gaze at the weeds and promise them...."Next year!"

And then it gets colder still. The first precious snow falls and I love that. I love it even more watching my girls love it. I frisk about between the car and the garage. When we do spend actual time outside, there are layers. So many layers and we slip and slide and fall when walking in it. Little Libby tries snow angels...but face down. I cannot help her up because I am laughing so hard I am crying. Later, we try hitching our huge dog Steve to the girls' sled. He pulls them like the Shepherd Husky Mastiff he is and even the neighbor kids get rides amidst peals of laughter.

Then more snow. Piles, weather reports and school closings. Cold. Brittle, painful cold. And just as I am tired of it, my friend Tess tells my little girls this story: "Everyone was complaining about the snow this morning, I felt grumbly about it until I looked around and saw it glittering! God gave me all this beautiful sparkling snow! I found it so beautiful, and I felt like a Fairy Snow Princess!" I smile at her sweetness, the joy and energy she has in telling her little story to my little people. Later that day, and the next and the next I, too, admire the glittering beauty and feel like a Fairy Snow Princess. I decided to be grateful for the beauty of it. I am grateful for our warm home, warm food and warm clothes.

And yet...I'm glad to see the snow melting. The dirty snow, the yellow snow, the icy snow. I look forward to mornings on our tiny porch, wandering the garden and ignoring the weeds. I drink coffee at the dinner table and I dream of the coming seasons.

DIE WHERE YOU ARE PLANTED

I have a deep, dark, brooding confession....I'm not good at keeping tiny things alive. And what I think a thing will be like may vary a great deal from reality. There is a movie that deals with rehab and when the people leave to go back to their real lives, the clinic has a suggestion. The person should try to keep a houseplant alive for a year before dating or making any other big changes. Well, I'm mostly sober and I can barely keep my houseplants alive. My beloved husband calls me a serial plant killer. About five years ago I confessed that although mentally I love having houseplants, my mother had tons of them, realistically I do not care for them well. I finally gave away all but three to someone with more space and active interest in keeping them healthy. It felt so great to stop pretending I could do better and just be honest with myself.

I then moved on to little creatures. While on vacation a few summers ago the hotel was selling little colorful painted hermit crabs in a cute little cage for $20. I thought it was a darling souvenir for us, the girls would love watching it and learning to care for him. He even had a bee painted on his shell and my dad is a beekeeper so it was perfect. We named him Buzzy. OH! I should add, I did have to sell the idea pretty hard to my husband … .and some of you are very clever and knew where this was going the moment I said "Hermit Crab".

My husband is dedicated to doing things The Right Way, which I deeply value and appreciate. As soon as we got Buzzy home, he started looking into the proper care and feeding of the little fellow. For those of you without your own painted hermit crab ownership story, let me share the $200 lesson we learned. Painted shells are hard on the little hermies. They like to have several natural shells to move in and out of as their inner fashionista desires. They are liars, and not all hermits prefer company. Unless they do not like each other in which case the little suckers become cannibals.

Oh yeah, they also want a particular warm temperature and humidity. And fresh water to drink and salt water to bathe in. They will want YOU to give them a bath once a week, too. And one may have to go to two different pet stores and buy a jillion stupid crabs before you give up, realizing that the original guy is in fact quite hermity, thank you. My dear husband ended up taking on 95% of the responsibility and care of the simple $20 souvenir I campaigned heartily to have. And after a year or two even Buzzy keeled over. I had him on the front porch in a box to have a service and bury him because our girls took it pretty hard...but then he started to smell bad and I ...uhhh made other arrangements. Our littlest daughter Libby asked again when we would have service for him just last week...he died about four months ago.

Maybe her memory was jogged when her goldfish died? You know the free prize goldfish from the school festival Goldfish Game. I'm pretty sure any of the cool moms serving in the PTO know before the carnival not to allow their children to play the game with the goldfish prize. My guess is the goldfish game is their revenge on the rest of us parents who hate PTO meetings. Of course I was new to all this when Portia was in kindergarten and I was not in the PTO. She and Libby played the game. A lot. And won. A lot. We went home with our goldfish prize. The prizes were coupons for what turns out to be fifteen cent feeder goldfish. Guess how much two small goldfish bowls, one bag of rocks, two decorations and food cost: sixty bucks. Thanks Goldfish Game. I'm already a grouchy, mean mom so I wasn't going to say no here. Maybe it would go well, you know?

We went through three rounds of goldfish deaths before we called it and gave up as fish owners. One bowl went to the basement and the other fishbowl became a terrarium for the five dollar flytrap plant on sale at Aldi. And yes, I realize if you want to be malevolent here; a flytrap is kind of a pet and a plant all in one. And I must admit it is not looking very good this week.

SIMPLE PLEASURE, DENIED!

I am embarrassed to admit this, but I am spoiled. Spoiled rotten and maybe a skosh lazy. And again, pampered and spoiled. Our front door is to blame for this revelation. We live in a lovely little bungalow from 1920 and all of the things do not work all of the time. This front door of ours actually still has the original doorknob and skeleton key slot. It is quite the physical challenge to close it, involving several slammings and a hopping leg dance to get the key to slide the deadbolt. Unless it magically locked on its own when you closed it a bit too hard. (An unreliable way to lock the door or lock yourself out of the house, directly related to how late one might be to get somewhere.)

So there's the door background story. This week the door got one over on us. On the edge of the door near the newer deadbolt and the original skeleton key situation there are two buttons of mystery. Some of you are grinning because you see where this is going. You already know what these buttons are. For the rest of you, Google ` ` old door lock buttons that can lock your door automatically via the skeleton key tumblers no one uses anymore because skeleton keys have gone the way of corded telephones and snail mail." That is what happened. Now our door is locked and we cannot open it. Our front door. The one we use daily, five thousand times a day.

We have ideas about how a button could have gotten pushed.   It wasn't me, of course. My daughters do not know anything about it but my husband did dislodge part of a butterfly hair clip from the skeleton key space. We have our ideas. I would call a locksmith because I am not handy and when I try to be handy, disaster and crooked shelves occur. My husband is brave and tinkered with the door and plans to tinker further. We will probably take it off of its geriatric hinges this weekend and hope that works.

Which brings me to this morning. This door stood between me and a hot cup of coffee on the front porch in the post thunderstorm freshness. I lamented out loud to my five year old Libby that I wish the door wasn't broken so I could sit on the porch. "You could go out the side door..." she stated, quite intelligent and alert even early in the morning. I said I knew that, but it was wet outside. "You could put on shoes," she said. We call her The Lawyer for a reason folks! Her ability to overcome my objections leads me to believe she could sell anyone anything, if law school doesn't work out.

I ended up wearing my husband's Crocs around to the front door. As I sat there enjoying my strong black coffee, I thought about how spoiled I am that the front door being blocked was a problem. I tried to enjoy the green trees and freshly mowed grass and my wisteria vine that is leafing out on the gate. I kept thinking about how many people in the world have real problems. About my friend who's husband is battling cancer and the dad at Libby's preschool who died tragically last month. I thought about all the arguments in our city over non-discrimination Human Rights Ordinance that people who never face discrimination said we didn't need. The fact that we still need to open a door in our cities to protect people from discrimination pains me. I thought about people in my neighborhood who do not have enough of anything: food, money, education.... closed doors of prosperity, locked tight to them. I am again reminded I live a Queen's life. I am spoiled and hope in the future when my simple pleasures are denied I will keep it in perspective.

There are many doors closed and locked in the world and I hope to remember this. My perspective changed even as I face the truth about my self-centered self. May I become a person who doesn't stand at a closed door lamenting an obstacle, but instead become a woman who finds a way around it, unlocks it or breaks it down.

VANITY OF A MIDLIFE CRISIS

The stereotype of a man's midlife crisis is a sports car or getting the earring they never had. Ewwww. Women tend to slide more gradually into our midlife. I suppose I shouldn't stereotype, so let me share my ugly slide towards middle age. I don't plan any plastic surgery, like ever. The best one liner I heard was a woman who said she wouldn't do that because she wanted her body to decompose when she died. My midlife crisis involves fake hair and neck skin, so hang on tight. And please take my picture from above, everyone knows that is most slimming for a selfie. Chin out, eyes up, camera above you just a bit....ready for that closeup!

As a teenager I was raised well, my natural appearance encouraged by my Father who always preferred a clean, makeup free face on a woman. What a wonderful message for a young girl to receive! I still dabbled in makeup and developed my love of a deep retro red lipstick. My Grandma taught me that some lipstick brightens the face so nicely. She wore a very optimistic pink and I still hear her in my heart whenever the topic of lipcolor comes up. In my 20's and 30's I wore makeup here and there but often had a bare face with the red lipstick center stage. I left my lip mark on cards, letters, bathroom mirrors and unwitting victims. Daily Lipstick carried me through adulthood beautifully until recently.

When I reached a certain age, it seemed my face began to change. I'd become accustomed to middle age post baby weight gain, and honestly did not care enough to fight back very hard, but my face! My skin! I began wearing makeup almost daily and spending more money on it. I'd start with just a little something and then keep adding because I felt so much better about how I looked. Then I noticed moisturizer wouldn't fix my neck. I thought it was just dry, and I won't admit here how much money I have spent experimenting with mid priced face and neck creams.

One day, amidst all of this vain struggle, I remembered the miracle of a falsie hairpiece. In my twenties I had a clip on ponytail. It was marvelous … .a waterfall of long shiny hair I could butterfly clip onto my teeny nub of a samurai ponytail. I would feel like a Victoria's Secret bombshell, a goddess, even with unwashed, unstyled hair. It took two minutes and I felt like a movie star. I still cannot explain it. I did however, in a rash act of humorous showmanship, remove my clip-on ponytail at work during a staff meeting.

I did it to demonstrate the dramatic "before and after" difference. I do not think they were impressed...more like amused horror. It wasn't a classy move, but aren't we all idiots in our youth?

My hair is fine and usually a dyed variation of auburn. I never grow it out well or long but have always coveted long, lustrous, full hair. My dream hair is long, red and curly. I once stalked a woman at a downtown South Bend event because she had my perfect hair. I asked if I could touch it, which I now know is creepy. Curly red headed Cathy Dietz and I became friends nonetheless.

Recently a new friendship led to an adventure at M&M Wig shop in Merrillville, Indiana. I found a fabulous ponytail clip to match my hair and immediately felt twenty years younger. I felt thinner and smarter and less like someone's frumpy mother. My new friend Kat also bought a clip on ponytail and soon we were posing in the preschool pick up line taking pictures of our fabulousness and giggling like middle schoolers. It was ridiculous and wonderful. So great.

I was embarrassed at first, and you may think I should be embarrassed still! I am a wild woman with intelligence, a fantastic life, friendships, deep faith and strong ties to my community. I still want to be pretty. I want to feel pretty. It gets harder for me to feel pretty and my suddenly bountiful hair is one way that works for me. If you see me one week with chin length hair, and the next week it's cascading down my back, just smile, wink and tell me I look beautiful. Keep the camera higher than my chin, and I am ready for my close up!

SPEAK PEACE

I am reeling lately from the social media frenzy of friends and fake news and divisive politics and all of the powerful words from a Martin Luther King Day workshop I attended at Valparaiso University. Forgive my fumbling through a few of these thoughts as I try to figure out how to find peace and live well in our current world and circumstances.

There were several insightful speakers and topics and my favorite was a man named Derrick Howard made a statement "When those who are not injured feel as offended as those who are, that is Justice". The idea is based on the Ben Franklin quote, "Justice will not be served until those who are unaffected are as outraged as those who are."

This little bitty sentence brought to my mind all the conversations I have had recently when my white, privileged friends express dismay about the political climate. They often beseech us all to "just get along", to "be positive", to accept things as they are. It reminds me of when a neighbor said she didn't see that we had any race relations problems in our city of Valparaiso. I said many other white, privileged people would agree with her and not be able to see the depth and breadth of racism around us. It has been easier to not see it in the past but it is a grave mistake to not see it now.

We are all racist. This is an idea I grappled with when I taught Fair Housing Classes for a property management company I worked for. We all see differences in each other including skin color and basic physical appearance. It is human and perfectly acceptable to see the difference, to have thoughts or personal opinions about the difference. What is troubling is when we believe and act as if those differences make us or them more or less of something.

Once upon a time ten years ago or so I was traveling for work and ended up at a Denny's. As I waited for my carryout order I looked over the patrons and was surprised by something unusual: They were all ugly. The people at Denny's were each fat or funny looking or old or toothless...I began to feel smug as only a twenty year old person can and amuse myself in my mind at their expense. Then it came to me that every single one of us is ugly. Me included. We can hide it, we can work through it, but at our core though we may be good folks, we can be ugly too.

I remembered this powerful and painful moment of personal development when Derrick Howard mentioned a quote he likes: "Ugly people know they are ugly when they wake up in the morning." He said most people know what holds them back in life. Most people know their ugly and pretty sides, and often this knowledge is where they speak and live from. He encouraged us by saying "Don't be ugly."

And so to my friends fighting on social media and to myself I say these things:

1) Do. Not. Be. Ugly. If I belittle someone and call them names no-one will want to hear my words. Our mothers were right: When we speak badly about another person it says more about US than them. Let's be mature adults and control ourselves.

2) Everyone should get a chance to be LISTENED TO. Yes, even Those People. Spend more time listening to other people and less time trying to speak our points. Let's ask them questions. Can we dig deeper with everyone's best interests at heart? In the safety of being listened to, they may be able to hear our words differently.

3) Do NOT slip into a cocoon with only like-minded people. YES we need to have our tribes, we need to feel safe somewhere in the world, but we cannot dismiss and close off the opposition lest they react the same way. Conversation in a bubble is worthless. Let's not block and unfriend folks. Doing that says our beliefs cannot stand against or beside opposing beliefs. (And If they cannot, are we sure we want to hold them?) I changed

my permissions to avoid some conflict and I took Facebook off of my cell phone to avoid the fray. This way I can participate in the conversations when I am ready instead of all day long.

I want to remember everyone wants to be liked and well thought of. I want to treat each person with whom I interact with love and grace and kindness regardless of how they interact with me.

A great lady recently said, "When they go low, we go high!" This is a challenging thing to do and takes strength. I want to be strong.

I want to be kind and stay involved. If I choose to be peaceful amidst daily challenges, my life will make a difference each day. I can do this: I can speak Peace.

WATER WARS

My family went to war this week with a neighboring house. We planned and prepared and plotted the attack. We are civilized people and we warned them, we did the chivalrous things and then we told them how it was. Although children should be shielded from all aspects of war, we used our innocent daughters to deliver the initial blow. They carried the formal written challenge in a Turkish letter scroll carrier made of metal carved with filigree and finesse. They chose matching dresses for their courier uniform. They crossed the street and knocked politely. (They did have to knock louder the second time, but they did not relent.) Our girls greeted the neighbor and stood outside after curtly stating "We will wait for your reply". The challenge was accepted. The time of battle was set for 1:00 pm July 4th, 2017.

You may realize I do not get out much. I'm not too fun, I like things tidy and I'm the kind of mama who tries to avoid a mess. I am a decent parent so I say "No" and "Clean that up" and "Eat your dinner, use your napkin why isn't your napkin in your lapstoptalkingwithyourmouthful!" I try to tip the balance in my favor occasionally. For example; I buy too many ice cream cones. We go out in pajamas. I bring home crafts and we fuss in the kitchen together. I also have a secret: I like a good water balloon fight.

I've purchased crummy cheap squirt guns that get ruined with sand at the beach, and we have struggled to fill water balloons at least once a summer. Then something happened: Some company called Zuru made instant fill & seal water balloon kits (and charged the equivalent of college tuition for them). I watched them in the stores all last year. Too much money for something that would essentially last five minutes and then need to be cleaned up. Everything changed when we made our bi-annual Costco trip and they had 350 water balloons for $20. The wheels began to turn and we declared war. Or I sent a text message anyway:

US: *R u around this weekend? There may be a family challenge pending.*

THEM: *Bring it. Down 1 kid so it's even numbers*

US: *The House of Rochon may be challenged by the House of Novak to a water fight within the next 24 hours.*

I also included a Bitmoji of myself as Wonder Woman that said "BRACE YOURSELF". (If you do not yet "BITMOJI", you might want to start!)

I sent text messages to some of our other neighbors alerting them to the battle between the House of Novak and the House of Rochon. I invited them to join in or to watch. Many of our neighbors make the effort to connect regularly in large and small ways and it feels good to really know my neighbors.

My husband started looking over the directions for the water balloons, another daughter brought a laundry basket upstairs to hold our squishy, bulbous weapons. My suggestion of running to Michaels for war paint was rejected. The breakfast dishes weren't going to wash themselves so I turned on Spotify and found the playlist "Epic War Songs for Glorious Motivation" and cranked up the volume. Dishes aren't exactly inspiring, but the music was.

Before long it was time to begin assembling munitions which included three mangy squirt guns in addition to our 350 Zuru water balloons in magic quick fill clusters. My husband had the proper wrist finesse to detach the filled balloons, so he did that while I used our kid's wagon to move laundry baskets of ammo across the street to our neighbors' neighbor's yard. We set six year old Libby as the guard of the goods. She sat in the wagon armed with a water balloon and a crummy squirt gun. She was impossibly cute and ferocious.

I made flower crowns for the Queen of both Households. We got a selfie with them, which is great because they were decimated within five minutes. I'd decreed the winner of this battle would be determined by which side was wettest and which crown was stolen first. The crowns were just gone almost immediately and the House of Novak fell to their foe wetly with plopping sound effects. There may have been a home court advantage in the form of a hose, but all is fair in love and war. The House of Rochon offered us losers some pretty great brownies with whipped cream. Brownies soften the sting of defeat. House of Rochon, prepare for a rematch...we can bring the brownies this time!

FULLY DRESSED

When I was young and single every day was an adventure of possibility; would I meet a cute guy? What would happen at that party? Would those new shoes hurt my feet? Nowadays as a middle aged mama and wife, my thoughts (if I have any at all) are more mundane: What could I make for dinner? Will my pants hurt by the end of the day? What the hell am I going to make for dinner?

I try to recapture the joie de vivre of my youth in little ways like buying clothes in an ambitious size, using glitter eyeshadow though I probably shouldn't and smiling at strangers. Because I am now officially a grownup, I usually shuffle through my day with a serious face, but I used to smile at everyone. Smiling is free and frankly, it is a size that fits, so I'm wearing one.

As a little kid I listened to records instead of the radio. Fiddler on the Roof, The Sound of Music, Michael Jackson Thriller and of course, Annie. I'd stand up on top of my dresser and belt out "Tomorrow" and "Maybe" and "You're Never Fully Dressed Without a Smile" written by Charles Strouse and Martin Charnin. I'd sing and smile and the world would be transformed. I need that now in my adult life.

I walk through the shopping center parking lot and grin and greet anyone in my path. They often look surprised when I speak to them. They wonder if there is something wrong with me, and usually they smile back. I feel like smiling at strangers is an easy way to cut through all the crap going on in the world lately. I don't know where to put my time or my money or my presence because there are so many things wrong and thanks to the internet I know about all of them and they all matter. I can't give money to everything, I cannot show up for every protest or meeting. So I pick what matters most to me. I spend money there and show up there. And I smile at everyone else because it is a small regular thing I can do no matter what else is on my twitter feed.

This smiling, it came into play last weekend when I was in Chicago with family and friends. We were slogging through the rain for a Lyric's Children's Opera. We whined and cried (not just me but the kids too) about our wet feet and hungry bellies and pouring rain. I talked with my kids about homeless people and rain and helping others. After the rain let up we slowed our pace and a young man stopped my Father on the sidewalk. His name was Dominick and he was well dressed with an untied bow tie. My dad was well dressed with a tied bow tie. Dominick asked my Dad to teach him how to tie his bowtie. He and his two gorgeous lady friends were dressed up heading to a wedding and he'd been looking for a bowtie-tier.

As our party of eight stood around their party of three on Michigan Avenue my Dad tied Dominicks' bowtie with as much care as he tied his own. I watched him, a tall older white guy, tete a tete with this young African American man in this intimate clothing moment. Man to man. Generation to generation. Race to race. It was a holy moment of love and instant friendship and I'm ashamed to admit I took pictures. I wanted to remember the small things that matter. That THIS was my America. That no matter what else was true, this moment was just as true. And I smiled. We all did.

KID CAMPING

With all the monstrous highs and lows for Americans these days, here is a crazy truth about our world: There is snow on the ground and people are camping in it for fun. You know, canvas tent-sleeping bag-peeing outside-heating up coffee on a firepit, camping. A local Boy Scout troop was snow camping just last weekend and my husband has shared a few stories about snow camping, but I do not see the appeal.

I like camping. Or I used too. When I was in my twenties my dog Darby and I would drive to Estes Park, Colorado every summer to stay at "Dreamland", our family cabin. It's an eighteen-hour drive so I'd camp one night each way. I felt like a badass traveling solo; setting and breaking camp, making a fire and eating what I could cook over it. Cheaper than a hotel, too!

When I got married, we put camping gear on our wedding registry and got it! Beautiful matching Eddie Bauer sleeping bags with plaid flannel inserts. A new Coleman Camp stove. A tent big enough for two adults and two dogs instead of my cute single girl pop up. We used the gear...once. Or Twice.

Then we had kids.

Some parents are awesome outdoors people who could manage taking little kids tent camping like my Dad. Other parents, like us, are just tired. We would occasionally admire our gear stowed in the basement. Once the girls were out of cloth diapers we even planned a camping trip most summers. We didn't go. We liked the idea of camping.

This summer some friends talked about camping. We even got serious enough to try reserving a spot but the campground was full. My friend Jen lives on the edge of our neighborhood park, so Lucas and I plotted to spend the night in her yard in our tents. It would be a hootenanny.

We dragged all the things from our homes to our makeshift campsite. Stuff was bought to roast on sticks. Our site hostess actually provided blow up mattresses for us. There would be three adults and five children camping. Our spouses opted for real beds in real houses. We razzed them, but since we were the more awesome parents, we would let them go home at bedtime. This was a mistake.

You see, the thing about camping is it looks fine as a concept. Some grownups do not fare well sleeping on the ground. Even with an air mattress, it isn't comfortable. I discovered one cannot move around because sleeping in what is basically a bounce house is noisy, awkward and no good. The bugs were too loud. I was somehow hot and cold at the same time. Our host's son went inside to his own bed right away, but our 8 year old daughters and two remaining 6 year olds were still awake and talking at 1:05am. My body ached from eating bags of salty chips. I'd lugged all this sssshload of stuff out here, so who am I to call "uncle!" and give in? When one of the five kids in the huge kid tent gets 'punished' by moving into your tent to sleep with you, you are punished too. Trying to yell at the other kids in the kid tent to be quiet without trying to get up off of the bounce house bed (or waking up the kid sleeping with you) is... impossible.

Then the other six year old moved into his father's tent. I think they might have slept. Around 2:10am I told Portia & Belle not one more peep. Guess what? PEEP. This sent Belle to her dad's tent too. We were like parental body snatchers. Five kids started the night in the big tent and now only one left. In the morning she was gone too, headed inside to sleep on the couch.

I hadn't slept and wondered how soon I could just give up, get up and go inside to make coffee. At 6:47 am I wearily decided I was only getting up and outta the tent one more time. Nature called, so GOOD MORNING. I staggered inside to make coffee and breakfast. As we recounted the experience and ate breakfast Jen said we should do it again soon. Bleary eyed and frazzled I grumbled, "Never, never, never again!". Later as we packed up our tents, deflated the mattresses and stowed the gear I began to think...."Well, maybe..." But never with snow on the ground. Or bugs. Or air mattresses...or children.

SCREEN FREE FRIDAY

We often tell ourselves stories that are not actually in the least bit true. I tell myself I am laid back. (Actually, Not. True.) I say I'm easy going(Nope. Actually, Quite Controlling.) I say we choose as a family to be UN Busy. And...that is partially true. I still feel too busy.

I'm trying meditation; the calm.com app is free and splendid. My daughters are less spazzy when they are doing even five-minute meditations. I'm trying to exercise. I use essential oils from the health food store to be mellower. I'm trying to get to sleep earlier...but actually... I found myself reaching for my smart phone all the time. As I started taking inventory of my time and tried to figure out how to get more out of my days with less in my days, I decided to fast.

Fasting sounds weird. It is usually a medical term where you don't eat or drink before tests or surgery. For the religious among us, fasting from food can be a spiritual process too. I will occasionally fast for spiritual reasons, avoiding food for a short period of time in order to focus on prayer. (Usually I just pray the time passes because all I think about is Cheetos and Diet Coke.)

It's practically Un-American to intentionally go without something...anything! I get some side eye when the topic comes up because depriving oneself on purpose feels...like deprivation.

I decided to take a random Friday as a Sabbath day of rest and retreat. I chose to fast technology by turning my cell phone 'off' and throwing a darling rooster apron from the Farmer's Market over my desktop computer. I posted my landline digits on Facebook for anyone interested and explained I would cease to exist for the day. Then I waited. I waited to see a total personal transformation. I waited to see what disaster would happen while I was out of pocket, out of touch.

Seven things happened. Seven times I lamented the lack of technology.

8:00AM I couldn't text my neighbor to borrow something. I'd have to walk or drive to her house...or in this case I waited till the next day & then texted her.

8:10AM I couldn't take a picture of my awesome Lipsense lipstick combination and post it. I wonder how the world is still spinning.

9:00AM I couldn't check the weather! I actually dug out the paper phonebook and called Time & Temperature. (Remember that?) It couldn't give me the hourly weather though, so I was unsure of when it would rain. I called my husband and he expressed disdain that I would put my tech free burden on him. He said I'd have to get my weather report the old fashioned way...but I reminded him the TV was included in my fast. He said the weather should be fine until mid afternoon.

9:08AM My friend called the landline to offer me her CSA for the week. We ended up TALKING. I felt like June Cleaver, sipping my coffee and having a telephone conversation. It was delightful and refreshing. If I'd had my smartphone on, it would have been two texts instead of wonderful conversation.

9:25 AM I worried my appointment might be late or need to check in with me.... then I resolved to just turn my phone on if she was 15 minutes late. She wasn't. She was right on time.

10:15 AM I wondered about the weather again. I didn't call my husband, but I wondered. And I couldn't meditate. My meditation is firmly tied to the app on my iPad. I just did some thoughtful meditation and breathing the old fashioned way. It was great, actually.

10:25AM There was an emergency where I needed to watch my friend's daughter, so I turned my phone on, kept it on silent, and when the girl's dad called to pick her up (4:00pm) he used my land line anyway, to honor my fast!

I ended my tech fast that evening to watch a movie with my family. My laundry was actually finished. The house was clean, and I'd read a magazine the day it came in the mail. I felt more relaxed, satisfied and accomplished than usual. It was like playing hooky from the world and I relished the peace of a simpler day. I was more aware of my dependence and addiction to technology and vowed to make fasting from technology a regular occurrence. Do you want to try your own fast? I'm doing it again next week, actually...

ALWAYS BE PREPARED

If you've always wondered how to make your husband's face contort into confusion, fear and amusement all at the same time, tell him you'd like to buy a gun. Especially if you already had one but sold it once you had children because it was just too risky to have it around. It is even more fun if during this conversation you use the words "Bug Out Bag" or the initials W.T.S.H.T.F. followed by 'bag'. Some of you are nodding, some of you have the same face my poor hubby had. In today's uncertain political climate, I just want to be prepared.

I read a book by author Steven Konkoly last year entitled "The Jakarta Pandemic" about a post apocalyptic/dystopian America where the hero has 'prepared' and keeps his family mostly safe and well fed. The author is a fraternity brother to John and also Navy Seal and began to get a following from the 'Prepper" community based on his thrilling fictional tales of world-wide woe. I ate up the story and had a clear picture of the suburban neighborhood in the book because it closely resembled one we lived in when freshly married.

I liked the book but did not start stockpiling goods or "preparing" because that is crazy. I might have even laughed when my local Costco offered thirty day emergency ration kits for a "low low price". Thanks to Costco we do have an admirable supply of diced tomatoes, dry pasta and Annie's mac & cheese. Useful in the event we are snowed in or too lazy to leave the house for a week. I know the U.S. Department of Homeland Security website www.ready.gov suggests we have enough supplies for at least 3 days without mobility or power. They have downloadable plans from FEMA and topics ranging from biological incidents to natural disasters. Our family's biggest move towards emergency preparedness was a case of bottled water. And of course the cans of diced tomatoes. We are a veritable fortress of Americana.

Lately I have been more curious about emergency preparedness. Thus the gun and W.T.S.H.T.F. Bag conversation. If you are a person who is interested in this topic, you may be called a "Prepper". If you are not interested, you think "Preppers" are crazy people digging holes in their backyard and kitting them out with camping gear and beef jerky. As I have been looking into all of the above, our clay dirt yard is too hard to dig into. I'm settling for a backpack of supplies we can keep in our basement. It does make sense to be prepared in case there is a storm and we lose mobility or power. No matter your thoughts on the 'apocalyptic end of days' scenario played out in many a good date night film, consider at least storing up the basics of extra food and water.

Now if your life is boring or the political climate around here has you nervous, you have lots of options. Steven Konkoly offers a secret book on prepping, "Practical Prepping, No Apocalypse Required" but it is not listed with his fictional best sellers.. As I began looking into prepping websites and books, it was fascinating and a little bit scary. My next trip to Costco I looked for and finally asked about the thirty day ration kit but it was no longer in stock. I bought nasty looking protein bars instead. I figured in an emergency we would be glad to have them and I wouldn't snack on them before then. If I got yummy granola bars the only emergency they would be good for is when we are out of cookies. So now we have bottled water and nasty protein bars.

I mentioned my interest in emergency preparedness to a perfectly reasonable friend of mine and her eyes got big, she grinned, and led me to her kitchen cabinet. She pulled out three foil sheets of bubbled tablets. I was confused until she explained she just ordered them online and if there was a nuclear 'event' a person was instructed to take one each day for three days and they flood your thyroid with iodine to keep radiation from wiping your thyroid out. I vacillated between pleased to learn a new tip and mortified that a perfectly lovely woman knew about such a thing. Was I right to be preparing if another normal neighbor also felt the need? Perhaps.

I told John about the iodine tablets and that I wanted to order them. He said if there was a nuclear attack on Chicago we'd be totally wiped out so there was no point in preparing. My face then screwed up into what I imagine was a horrified mirror of his face when I brought up getting a gun. He agreed we would do a little at a time, that it was good to be prepared. I told him to spare me honest details about our chances. I said in any disaster what people need is hope. I don't know if I won that conversation, but I'm heading to the basement soon to try out those canned tomatoes. And maybe a protein bar.

HOW'S YOUR BUCKET?

I've been struggling to find joy lately. I took the Facebook app off of my phone so I could control my exposure to...All The Things. I am staying engaged, I am in the resistance, but I need to keep myself balanced and encouraged. I look for big ways to make an impact. I am in groups and I am writing letters and I am making calls. I marched in a local women's march. I am doing what I can to be positive but it is hard and I am often afraid.

Recently on the walk through our neighborhood to school, I was humbled and inspired by my seven year old daughter Portia. She might pretend she is a ninja instead of unloading the dishwasher the fourth time I ask, but Man! She can deliver a sermon without preaching.

One of her friends, Isabel, was having a crummy day and it was affecting the mood of our little "walking school bus" enough that I just started walking way ahead with a few kids to avoid it all. I saw that Portia lingered back with Isabel and her father, Lucas, who is one of my favorite people. I kept going, not wanting to deal with the fray. I was annoyed and dismissive. Lucas came up to me and said "Portia is talking about Bucket filling?" I stopped still on the sidewalk. Tears filled my eyes and I began to explain.

Not too long ago my family was in town to visit my Dad and we attended the Unitarian Church I grew up in. The children's moment there consisted of a dear lady named Cathy Duncan reading the book "Have You Filled a Bucket Today? A Guide to Daily Happiness for Kids" By Carol McCloud. The author talks about how everyone had a desire to be loved and appreciated and we carry around a 'bucket' of feelings. When we make someone else feel good, we fill their "bucket". If we are unkind to someone we are dipping into their bucket and taking away their good feelings. The book said some people try to fill their own bucket by taking from others, but it never, ever works well. I find that many messages like this given to children are often even better aimed at adults. We need it more!

My daughters talked about being "bucket fillers" for weeks after they heard the story. They looked for ways to help others, to apply the message. I talked about it with my mentor and she gave me her copy of the book since her kids had outgrown it. We thrilled together at the power of this positive concept. I shared the book with my friend Karyn who leads our church's Childrens' Ministry and they liked the message so much they used the entire "Be a Bucket Filler" curriculum for weeks! Many of us got our buckets filled by the kind words and actions of the kids learning to look for ways to fill other people's buckets.

So back to the sidewalk. There I was, supposedly every inch an adult, dismissing a little kid having a hard day. I wanted to avoid the tantrum, their sad feelings, their littleness. I was guarding myself from it (and besides there was a parent there to deal with her). My daughter did better. My daughter engaged her friend with love, distracted her, and told her about bucket filling. As Portia's kind and patient words lifted Isabel's heart, I saw at once how effective this was. We all started telling Isabel nice things about herself. We told her what we admired. We told her what we were proud of her for. We all begin smiling. We walked together and started telling the other kids in our group how they mattered, how they made us smile, how glad we were to know them.

We were all lifted up, smiling, energized and full of joy. Filling each other's buckets filled our own lumpy and battered buckets. A little child had to lead us, but she changed the course of our morning. Instead of dismissing someone's pain, she worked around it to fill a bucket and changed the world. Her corner of it, anyway.

18 FOR 2018

So...we have this shiny new year. We are only a little bit into this 2018 and we hold our breath against the anguishes we knew in 2017. We pray and we hope and we cast spells or throw dishes or journals until there are no pages left. Good people we know die. Others experience pain so rocking and deep we cannot even. We do not know what to say, or do or...we sit like Job's friends around them in silence, just being there. Or we avoid them. Sometimes we wish we could avoid ourselves. We make mistakes and try to improve our lives and ourselves and here we are again in the daily struggle and challenge and bittersweet of life.

So we have this shiny new year and we are desperate for it to be better. We want to be better. Resolutions? New Year's Resolutions? They can fall flat by mid March. Some of us are old enough that we know ourselves well enough to skip that old saw. At least this year. This year matters! For those of us who are the list makers, the do-ers, the ones who used to enjoy a good resolution or two— I have something interesting to share.

That Gretchen Rubin author I mentioned

before, on her "Happier Podcast" she mentioned "18 for 2018" in several episodes. It was a listener's idea about making a bucket list for the year. It has normal, personal resolution-y goals like losing weight, but more measurable like "lose 10 pounds and weigh 'x' amount". The "18 for 2018 List" contained long term goals of personal improvement (like quest for and land a more satisfying job), but also things we just want to do that make us happier. It was a combination of 18 items that would make you happier in the next twelve months, from small to huge.

I started jotting things down for myself in my Passion Planner like "take a random road trip" and "use old time swear words instead of cussing so very much you work in a church for crying out loud.". I added to the list and felt so inspired I have my '18 for 2018' AND a bunch of alternates. I have already crossed a few off: 13) 'Get a museum membership' and 16) 'purge old cosmetics'. I've started on 'lose 5, 10, 20 etc. pounds' by joining Weight Watchers and going to the YMCA a few times each week. I've seen 4 of 14)"Watch all 26 Marilyn Monroe Movies''.

My husband, who is neither a resolution maker nor a journal-er joined me in making a list of his own. Our friends have put pen to paper and compiled their lists with lovely action items and thoughts. We are becoming more intentional about our time. We want to be present, mindful, satisfied in the smallest parts of our days. We are sharing our lists and connecting more deeply with each other as we name and share what matters to us; 9) Plan a girl's weekend and 12) read two poetry books and 1) Learn how to do a headstand.

Other people's items are inspiration for more of my own: Host a high tea. Celebrate Galentine's Day. Help my child succeed in their hobby. Attend live sporting events. Volunteer monthly doing I.T. or greeting or filing or being a tutor. Run a 5k. If this list idea interests you, what would be on your list? The act of naming a thing can be powerful for our minds. Creating our lists and posting them visibly can steal back time from the little foxes nibbling away at our hours and days.

It is easy to believe that deeper joy and better lives lie in buying newer things, in being thinner or having that corner office. The truth is whatever we already have becomes old and doesn't satisfy us for long. Being intentional with our days and weeks and years can help us be happier with more life in our life. We are not guaranteed time here. Even this simple moment together is a gift. What will you do with this shiny new year?

PARDON ME

We are all so gross. You are, I am, that guy at your work is. You know it is true. You know how sometimes a person...I'm not saying YOU of course, but a random person might get a thing on their whatever? Like lint or a booger or leftover food from their last meal....it's on their thing and they do not know. Don't we have a social obligation to tell them? I mean, wouldn't you want to know? Sure it is embarrassing as all get out that my eyeliner has smeared or my lipstick has crusted but I'd rather know since everyone else will.

My Husband has this funny little game he plays with me. When I happen to notice (and I always notice) that he has a blemish or shmutz or a stray hair, I tell him. I want him to fix it remove it pull it wipe it so that I can continue admiring his radiating good looking manliness. Guess what he does? NOTHING. He leaves it there because it drives me insane, and he loves that. At first I didn't catch on. I thought he didn't hear me. Oh, he heard me. If you are laughing, you may well be another person who plays this game and I hate you just a little bit because I cannot hate my hubby. Sometimes after I've tried to...uh...help him, a little bit more attentively, he really goads me. He'll grin big with spinach in his teeth and lean towards me for a kiss. He'll leave whatever it is, wherever it is, to show me who is in charge. I get him back by telling my radio friends about it on the public radio airwaves.

Which camp are you in? Are you a grossness pointer-outer or are you grossness-oblivious? My guess is if you are, like me, always finding the little imperfections daily humanity offers, you are probably also Type A. You like all the things just how and where you like them. If you aren't critical like us Type A folks, you may not only enjoy life around you more than we do, but also...you probably leave all of life around you! I find myself not just fussy in little personal nuances, but in other areas too. I can find fault with anyone anytime, even if I work hard to fight that immediate reaction. I am critical, and often see how anything could be better. My main struggle these days is fighting the urge to express these views unless someone asks for my opinion. Most people do not really want another person to point out their weakness or shmutz or to offer a better way to do everything. It is all relative.

I think this behavior of mine comes from my Dad. You may have heard me say we call him the VOA or Voice of Authority. He can tell anyone how to do anything...even if he himself has never done the particular thing. He isn't doing it in a jerky way, actually, he does it with great love. I realized long ago he only wants everyone to have the best experience possible. He wants the best for all of us. I do too.

The trouble with a critically 'helpful' worldview is that a person living this way can spend all of their energy on other people and not enough on their own details. I for example can get critical about an un-emptied out sink drain even though the dishes were washed(and not by me!). BUT I am easily able to ignore the clean folded laundry basket I need to put away for days...even weeks. I won't get my butt to the gym, or prep for a meeting or pluck my eyebrows...but you've got stuff in your thing. You should take care of that immediately.

JUST LOOKING

Sometimes a person wants a big change. Life can get too easy or predictable. I've been married for 11 years to my handsome husband. We have two kids, one dog, two guinea pigs and a fifteen cent goldfish that could survive a nuclear bomb. I love my life but wanted something new. I wanted something younger and more exciting and so I did what anyone in my situation would do: I went online. Pictures say a thousand words and I spent several weeks swiping left or swiping right looking for that special someone. Before you judge me, you should know my husband was into it.

It was mostly my idea but obviously he had to like them also; the look, age, build and weight of them. Chemistry for both of us mattered...and so I'd send pictures to him, we'd talk and we'd set up a meeting.

We weren't in a hurry but I wanted to find the right one before May 11th. On that date Steve would turn twelve years old. Steve is our Shepherd, Husky Mastiff mix dog. I wanted to find that special someone for Steve's birthday...someone new to add excitement into our daily lives and serve as a backup for him as he ages. Steve was my dog Darby's "Birthday Present" when she was aging. I'd heard getting a puppy for your senior dog could be a good thing. The puppy offers energetic companionship for the old dog, and also learns a trick or two. I don't know if Darby appreciated the puppy, but she went along with it. I like this model of pet acquisition better than losing a beloved pet, having a gaping hole in your world and then just replacing them with a new model. Having the two pets together feels easier, sweeter.

So as I said, we looked online. We'd admire pictures on Petfinder and if there was enough chemistry we would meet. Adding to your family is always a weighted decision. I knew any young dog would need a lot more of everything. At first I fell for Freya. She was a really different dog, a 4-month-old Saluki mix I'd never heard of. I loved her story and applied for her. We met her at a Rescue Event the next day and found out the rescue wanted $350, three personal references, a vet reference, a home visit and a meet and greet with our current dog. WHAT?

I bought Darby from a Chicago pet store for $75. Steve was a 'free to a good home' fellow from down the street. I have a friend who fosters for a rescue and I thought that was the route we wanted to follow. We jumped some hoops but the process was too stressful and it felt like they didn't actually want to adopt out the dog. Sadly we moved on.

Lulu was cute. She was an Australian Shepherd at the Humane Society and was so endearing and desperate to be loved. We met her and put in an application. As the staffer told me our application wasn't the winner, she shared that her family met eight dogs before they got one. WHAT? NOPE.

The tension of searching for a dog that felt right, meeting them, considering their impact on our family and then asking to be approved to adopt was awful. I seriously doubted that "Rescuing" was the right route. We began to hear stories where fosters really did want to just keep the dog. Most of the dogs weren't right for us. After weeks of tears and frustration I wanted to give up.

Finally my friend Meg sent me a Petfinder link for a cute one-year-old collie mix named Cassie. I showed her to John, he liked her so we clicked the button requesting more information. Cassie was fostered through Rover Rescue in Illinois. While two hours from our home, we'd found a rescue that actually placed dogs in homes! If we met her, and everything went well we would bring her home. That is exactly what happened!

Cassie is a lively, super sweet girl and we love her. She is the perfect dog for us. She and Steve rollick and rumpus in marvelous play. Life is surely more interesting now! Earlier today Cassie demolished an almost empty bag of bread left on the counter and she happily brought us an unscathed chapstick as we sat on the couch. She's perfect. Happy Birthday, Steve?

RIDE A BIKE, CHANGE YOUR LIFE

Do you wish you lived somewhere else? Do you want some fabulous life change to shake up your days: More money, an adventure, new job, new house, new town? Do you want something (anything) different? I bet lots of us wish we could escape the dull ebb and flow and status quo of our daily life. (Parents, can I get an amen since we add fanny wiping and the stress of littles to our daily rhythm?) What if you could make some life change happen in a magical way right now?

Am I snorting fairy dust? NOPE. You can. For example....I want to live in Colorado. I love the breathtaking views, lots of my family is there and our family cabin too. I also love the healthy atmosphere and lifestyle living in Colorado offers. BUT: We have family here too. John has a great job and we have good friends and our parents nearby so moving away is not a great option anytime soon.

When I first moved away from Denver, Colorado and realized on a trip back how much I missed it, I asked myself some questions about what exactly I missed. I think a lot of the time what we THINK we want, simply has some components in it that look like how we want to live. If we can discover that and recreate that for our life NOW...WOWZA!

For me, one of the facets of the Colorado lifestyle I envy is bicycling. At the time I lived in South Bend and worked in an office about eight miles from my house. I decided that even though I didn't live in Colorado I could live like I do and bicycle to work. It involved a bad hair day, wet wipes and a shirt change...but I did it! I was so thrilled and scared and proud of myself. I biked to work through a non-bike friendly city several times. It was an adventure, a conversation starter, fun and it allowed me to change my life now instead of waiting for someday to come.

Then kids happened. Well marriage first for me, then the kids, then the move to Valparaiso, Indiana. Still in the area, one hour closer to Colorado, but not quite there. I got a bike trailer from my husband for Christmas two years ago and the kids didn't love it right away. Poor Libby was all head and helmet and too little to even be able to turn her head. It was hilarious in that Yes-I-Laugh-AT-My-Kids kind of way.

Last year it was better. The girls started to enjoy the ride. I was adventurous...we didn't just go around the neighborhood, people. We ran errands: Without A Car. In a somewhat bike friendly city this time, but still. Drivers aren't aware of bikes and I have to be vigilant and often (sorry!) ride on sidewalks. I'd rather run over a pedestrian than have the girls and I hit by a car...a mama has priorities.

Today wasn't a humid day and not too warm, so we biked again. Libby and I biked Portia to VBS, then we headed to Target, Bath and Body Works and Sally Beauty Supply. We waved at helpful drivers, rang our bell at other bikers, walkers and folks in their yards. We saved money on gas, took great care of the environment, got great exercise and enjoyed life at a slower pace. Wonderfully rewarding despite the sweaty shirt.

This works for us. Maybe it isn't your thing but could help you pinpoint something that will add excitement and adventure (or even life change) to your days. What is your version of life change? We all want more fun and more adventure in our daily lives....what do you want to try next?

BIRTHDAY MONTH

Have you heard? It is my BIRTHDAY! Well really it is my birthday month, or it was anyway. Still is, if I haven't gotten cake with you on the calendar yet! After becoming a mama, I moved my traditional Birthday Week into a Birthday Month because...KIDS. As a parent, my needs are often overlooked in lieu of raising awesome young people. I kind of have to get an appointment with my own Dad to not have our conversation overruled by the epic cuteness of my two daughters. But, the more birthdays I have, the more furtive I feel about them, not the "ME! ME! ME!" of it, but the...number of it.

I told my husband years ago that after hitting a certain age and feeling literally and figuratively "Old" that I was going to start fibbing my age. He said "You don't lie about anything else in your life, why on earth would you do that?" I said it just made me feel old when I saw a certain range of numbers.

I wanted to feel fabulous....and so instead of my age I opt to say "Fabulous" when asked my age. Now that I have watched the first season of The Marvelous Mrs. Maisel, I'm changing my reply this year to "Marvelous". "How old are you?" and I say "Marvelous, thank you!"

This year, in step with not acting my age, I've had a five year old's birthday theme: UNICORNS. I appreciate the beauty and silliness and whimsy of unicorns like everyone else in America, apparently. I think we all want and need to avoid reality. Unicorn and mermaid themed stuff is everywhere, and
my darling friends and family made sure I got most of it. From glittery Unicorn Dust, a rainbow water bottle and a coffee mug....I am magical as can be. My own perfectly reasonable hubby got me a pink
sparkly unicorn poncho just to make me laugh.

I think one of the best ways to feel young is to remain interested in small simple things. Being silly and inviting others to join in the playful with me spreads my sense of joy. I am not afraid to look foolish; I revel in it. Putting down the burden of worrying about what others will think makes my days
a lot happier. (No one actually thinks that much about me, anyway.) It is freeing to just be who I'd like to be.

There is one gift I received from several people this year that I love, but also fear: Dish

Towels. Dish towels? Oh sure, they are lovely and witty and funny and creative … .but….they belie my true age.They admit for me that I have everything I want and need. That I have in most ways "Come of age".

The towels started before my birthday."I Love Jesus, but I Cuss a Little" came first, from my mother in Love. She said it was so funny she couldn't wait until my birthday to give it to me. Spot on. Then the hot pink one from another friend said "Sometimes I just want God to say 'YO! I like You Best'." Later, I got a white towel with a pig outline and it said "Praise the Lard", because I like bacon more than a little bit. Then "I don't have my ducks in a row, I have squirrels, and they are DRUNK!" on a reasonable gray/beige "greige" background. The last one, so far, was "PMS=Pass the Merlot, Sister!"

It is true that I need new dish towels. Half of the ones I own are from when I married John twelve years ago. It is great to add some humor into my kitchen. But. I am at some unwritten age, some matronly place where I do not need anything else and where the witty dish towel is to be expected. I am embracing this linen filled moment. I am grateful to add another year to my life and amused at the generosity and creativity of the people I adore around me.

I guess the only thing that can be done is to get down off of this unicorn and wash some dishes.

GOOD UGLY

Many of us have a bit of vanity and as we age and wrinkles show up we either give up and go with it (which I think is healthiest) or we start buying those $200 neck crèmes and trying botox. At my solid age of...'marvelous' ...I am grateful to be a good ugly. I say good ugly because my face has had a Bell's Palsy adventure I do not wish upon any of you. Being uglier has taught me many things I'd like to share.

If you do not know, most do not, Bell's Palsy is a mystery. It is a disease that makes your face look like you are having a stroke. Half of your face becomes paralyzed and it can last weeks, months, years or never heal completely. I headed to the ER on March 11th apologetically explaining I thought I was having a stroke. They did the scans and the tests and diagnosed Bell's Palsy. I've only heard of that from author and speaker Rachel Hollis who has had it several times. (I KNEW I was just like her!) I was given a pile of prescriptions and went home to Google myself into a panic.

I won't bore you with it all. You, too can google. I'll share that I had trouble eating, my affected side eye wouldn't close so I wore unsexy eye patches and I felt like garbage for two months. I didn't work and actually couldn't even visit with friends or talk on the phone because even 20 minutes of conversation wore me out. My face had to compensate for the paralyzed side and would ache terribly.

I am a person who talks for a living. I do motivational and keynote speaking, I am active in my work at church welcoming and connecting people. My smile and red lipstick is who I say I am to the world. My spark felt extinguished. I grew depressed. I slept a lot. I did all of the therapy Blue Cross and Blue Shield could buy: massage, physical therapy, acupuncture. I drank organic juices, slept, avoided stress and cried at my ugly face. I got dozens of sweet get well cards and beautiful gifts and soup. A facebook Group for facial paralysis was a valuable group for me. At one point early on I learned to apply my red lipstick unevenly so that my mouth would actually look more even.

When I spoke, children would stare and adults would give double takes. I looked weird and realized people would think I was...what? Less than? Developmentally disabled? Ugly? Would I be dismissed? Had I dropped from the good place in life I held as an educated, somewhat attractive white woman into...normalcy? Was I below normal now? Instead of completely panicking, I saw this as a gift. I could see what it was like to be treated differently.

I started to watch how people interacted with me. For ogling kids I immediately said "Isn't my face crazy? This side is paralyzed and lazy! Can you grimace-smile like this?" It broke down the barriers for them (and their parents) and I was able to educate. When I saw people out in public who were ugly like me, or had something "other" about them, I observed them. I tried to grimace-smile reassuringly and knew that their mind could be just like mine on the inside. I worked harder for my words to connect with people since my smile was gone. Without the light in my eyes conveying warmth, I looked a bit scary when I tried to smile.

Feeling trapped in my broken face reminded me we are all people who matter. We all want to look nice and be liked and we all have something to give the world. I believe I am kinder and more patient with strangers than before Bells' Palsy made me a good ugly. I gave up waiting for my face to get normal again and decided I had too much to do to wait for healing. I started working again as I felt stronger. I spoke more, I wrote more. I thought more about what I wanted to do with my life, with this whisper of time I have to be alive and connect with other people. I thank God for letting Bell's Palsy happen to me, for making me a good kind of ugly.

Now I have some slight movement in my face coming back after four months of struggling and I'm grateful. I'm thrilled to see eye wrinkles because it means my mouth is getting the smile muscles working all the way up through my cheek. I'm excited to maybe wear eye makeup again soon and feel prettier...and I will never forget this good ugly life lesson from Bell's Palsy.

NEIGHBORHOODS

The domicile in which I live has always been important to me. I grew up on Troy Court in South Bend Indiana, then Alpine St., Twyckenham and then Emerson Ave for most of high school. I moved out a bit early (a bit young but needing to escape family struggles), into a furnished second story apartment above a house on Pleasant Street. I lived on both 8th and 9th streets in Mishawaka, and on Columbia St. in South Bend by the post office when it wasn't charming. I've lived in Chicago and Denver and South Bend again on Altgeld Street and then MacArthur Ct. Now Valparaiso, Indiana. With every move, the selection of space had two requirements aside from being affordable: walking distance to something edible or doable, and it had to feel good.

Like many of you, I adore hardwood floors. I want quirky. I've never lived long term in an apartment with carpeting and a dining area. Not everyone cares about enjoying or decorating their living space, but those of us who do know what I mean when I say it has to feel good. Many times I would ask to be alone with the space, and just sit on the floor and be present. I'd notice the light, or the openness; I'd listen to the sounds and think about my things and where they would fit. I made several realtors pull out their hair when I would walk into a house and know instantly it was not right for me. I've had an unusual ratio of delightful oversized clawfoot tubs in my powder rooms, even in two of my apartments. Also, lots of hardwood floors and the one time I didn't, I got permission to rip up the sad brown carpet myself. Beneath was terribly distressed wood and I coined my personal version of "Cottage floors' and left them as is.

I like to have food nearby, because I eat it often. I've had a greasy spoon diner, Greek restaurant, 7-11, the old Cira's, Bob's 19th Hole, and Zephyr's Ice Cream parlor near my places. I love exploring neighborhoods! I've enjoyed geocaching as a way to find nooks and crannies hidden to others. I usually have a dog and walking with them uncovers a whole new world of slowing down to sniff everything, to chat with other people walking their dogs (we only exchange the dog's names, tho?). I notice little things I'd drive by altogether too quickly. We now live half a mile from our city's downtown, and we love to wander as a family or individually to meet a friend or take in entertainment or just run errands on foot instead of by car.

I've grown to treasure how much more life happens when I walk through our neighborhood. At 5:30am, I meet other neighbors as they walk their dogs or head out for a run. As a family, we might walk to see a friend in the neighborhood, or stroll after dinner with the dogs saying hello to everyone we see. We talk about happenings in town, local meetings of interest or concern and each other. We share the news and politics and who moved in or out. My daughters and I walk to and from school most days in a walking school bus of friends and neighbors. It is one of my favorite things, coffee mug in hand, to walk far enough behind them I might as well stay home, but I want to see my friends, too. Parenting hacks are shared, and excess tomatoes, baked goods, love.

Recently we walked to the end of our street with dinner for a new mom. It was hot and I wasn't thrilled, but unfortunately I have taught my daughters to avoid using our car when possible. We care about the environment and make good efforts to walk or bike and this time they voted to hoof it. We carried dinner and a gift, and when we arrived another neighbor was there too. We took turns holding the baby, eating the rotisserie chicken and slaw salad and hummus. My friend Amy's heart is more Kenyan than American and I admire her simple approach to new motherhood. Her home was peaceful, warm, and had hardwood floors of course. Her husband Edwin was mowing the lawn, and then came in to hug, and eat, and smile. Their house, like ours, is smaller...and it doesn't need to be any different. We were at peace together.

Good neighborhoods aren't about big fancy houses; they are about the people living together in the same place, the same streets. What makes the places I've lived better or less than, are the connections I've had to the people around me. The place I live in matters because I want to invite people into it. The neighborhoods I've lived in and walked through have more value when I've walked from front yard to doorstep, person-to-person, friend-to-friend. My life is good because of hardwood floors and yet another claw foot tub... but the people living around my pretty house are what make me feel at home.

MUG STORIES

I have a question to ask you, friends...and all of you can answer this one, probably without too much embarrassment: How many coffee mugs are in your kitchen cabinet at this moment? When this sentence formed in my mind I realized I would have to answer it myself: I have eighteen mugs in the cabinet and one on the counter, dirty. I honestly do not know how my mug number reflects on me. What is the average number of mugs in other people's cabinets? We have a tiny kitchen and there is truly no room for one more mug, but I am loath to part with them. Each mug tells a story. Each mug carries memories of people and love and moments of coffee, tea, cocoa. Can you relate? I wonder what your mugs whisper about your lives even now?

I married into some of them, of course. One has a Garfield cartoon where Odie the dog is dressed up with hearts and an arrow. The obese orange tabby says "I asked for Cupid, not Stupid!" (Poor Odie!) My young daughters like this one the best. The creamy white one with the thick lip edge and floral motif is also my husband John's. It is his mom's special mug she uses for tea when she is here. The Shutterfly 'Dad Mug' we crafted for my hubby with our little family depicted in goofy little family pictures all around it. But there are others. There are other mugs telling deeper stories.

There is the Black Krispy Kreme Donut mug my friend Jean bought me on a road trip to Ohio. We stopped at the place so she could introduce me to what that HOT sign really meant. I'm afraid we killed half a dozen donuts right then and there. And she bought me the mug. Another time when she went to New York she brought me the white mug, this one from Dean and Deluca's. I've never made it to New York and I don't know Dean or Deluca but the mug is special to me. The Chicago Diner mug that I got from my Dad one Christmas is in there. I received it along with a (vegan) Chicago Diner cookbook that year.

My mug stories are not all so light hearted. There are a few mugs I hold tightly to. The ones I would weep over if they were ever lost or broken. The brown glazed one with painted bird shapes on it. The blue and gray patterned one with a brown edge. The cheesy red 'LOVE' mug with words for love in different languages is my least favorite. These are mugs my mother drank from when I was a child. She drank coffee, tea, spiked eggnog and weekend bloody marys from them. She tipped the mugs to her lips with wine, with vodka in orange juice, with anything she thought she was hiding booze in. Eventually she got help and quit drinking alcohol. My mother drank from these three mugs until I was thirteen. She stopped drinking anything out of them because she died.

I can close my eyes and see her sitting on a gaudy yellow couch with black stripes like a cartoonish bee. I remember her wonderful laughter, our frank mother daughter talks about anything. I remember feeling so many things as I processed her presence and then her absence in my life. And I have these mugs. They remember my stories, my history, for me.

I usually drink coffee from them. I have made a hot toddy at times to fight off a cold. I offer them to my daughters, to my friends who visit, often holding my breath against accidental destruction. I want to share them, I love to invite a friend to select their mug from the cabinet themselves. I watch them ponder and sort and I notice their choices. I risk a mug my mother drank from accidently crashing to the floor because I do not need the mug to remember. I hand them out like any other mug because I need to let go of anything too precious to share with a friend.

What are your mug stories? My newest mug makes me laugh when I use it. My friend Thais found a quote that encompasses my life perfectly. She made me this special mug for Christmas with the quote on it. I brandish it proudly: "Somewhere between Proverbs 31 and Tupac, there's ME!"

CANINE CONNECT

I have always considered myself a B+ pet owner. I don't follow the year round flea and tick treatment and I don't have my dog's teeth brushed by the vet under sedation. My pets usually come to me free or through a rescue so we aren't high end on that end either. But I love them. And I love a lot of them. I was raised as a child amidst a menagerie of cats, dogs, parakeets, tanks of fish and one short-lived guinea pig whos' funny munching on cat litter shortened his lifespan: immediately! (I think I've been trying to make that up to his ghost with all three of the guinea pigs we've had these most recent years!)

Of all my pets, I find myself most amused with our newest member: Cassie. She is the dog we rescued for my 13 year old dog Steve's "birthday gift". And perhaps we are A+ pet owners now, as we pay large dollars for two surgeries and medicine to keep Steve healthy and happy. Our precious ninety-five pound Steve with glossy a black Husky/Shepherd coat and gangly Mastiff legs. He is so handsome we get stopped on the street. Even the children in our neighborhood flock to Steve first, then to little Cassie as an afterthought.

Cassie is not an afterthought during our training classes. She is accidentally the center of attention as she looks like a million dogs. We try to figure her out, my friend Meaghan, the trainer Laura, others. I want to get her DNA tested, a luxury available to us in this indulgent pet owner day and age. I've no idea what she is, even as I learn who she is. She is the sweetest dog I've ever known. Even beating out my first dog, Darby who climbed mountains in Denver and sat beside me in dog friendly bars in Chicago. Cassie is skittish and also fiercely protective. I am afraid for her because I fear she might like to bite.

We began taking training classes at a Dog Sports place in Valparaiso, Indiana called Canine Connect. We take small classes with only my friends' small dog and one or two other hapless fur babies trying to sit, stay and walk loose leashed. On the plastic turf amidst tunnels and cones and jumps we stayed only on the flat ground. We worked giving more treats than I thought we should. Treating and rewarding and saying "YES!" every time our dog looked at us as master.

Cassie would lunge at other dogs near her, but her body language didn't say anger. She had to meet a person before they reached for her or she would indeed try to nip...but once properly introduced she was a love. How could I properly (and safely) introduce her to the swarms of children on our walks to and from school? How could I reassure her the world was mostly safe and full of joy? She had been wounded, we think. By man or beast or both. She wanted to love, to please, but she had learned to protect herself too.

One week our trainer said she would become more confident with training and not be so fearful. A few weeks later, the same trainer said she should see a behaviorist, and that we might not be able to train her out of her wariness. I felt offended and ashamed of my little pup. She was desperate to get things right, to please me. She adored my husband and the girls, never making us nervous for our safety. I remained anxious about her when people came over, or when we walked. I'd have her sit and ask people not to reach for her, to pet Steve first and then let Cassie come up to them. I explained she was timid and afraid (that felt better than warning them she might bite).

Lately in class we used obstacles and Cassie has become a Superstar! She goes through the tunnel, over the jump returning to my right or my left depending on my hand gesture. She sits close to other dogs and behaves well. She has an easier time meeting people on the street and behaved well when people poured into my home for a coffee date recently. I feel confident that Cassie is improving after all. While she will absolutely guard her family, she is learning to trust and settle next to me instead of lunging towards an imagined enemy. We intend to keep taking our classes together forever. During our most recent class, she finally jumped on top of an exercise ball and stood there, uneven in her footing as it jiggled beneath her, her eyes on me for reassurance. I was so proud! Cassie Jyn, like my Darby, Our Steve, is an A+ dog all the way.

ACT YOUR AGE

Act my AGE? No thank you. At the breakfast table recently, I got corrected for using the word "Yo." I don't know if it was embarrassing for me to use it because I'm middle aged, or not hip, or if it is not hip to say "yo"... I'd listened to the Fresh Prince song "Parents Just Don't Understand" by accident and "Yo" felt like the right choice at the time. Beastie Boys were also in rotation because I remember my wilder days and feel younger. It might feel a little mid life crisis, but I do not want to grow up and be an adult.

Parenting is the fastest way to grow up-and old-without noticing it. Being completely in charge of little people's lives is draining. I eased my 'adulting' pain the first time when I had this epiphany of "What kind of parent do I want to be?" I'd been grouchy all day and I finally decided to ask my kids, both preschoolers at the time, what they wanted in a mommy. I was getting big life thoughtful with little kids. I wondered did they want me to be crafty? Scholarly? I bent low to their little faces and asked, "What kind of mommy do you want darlings?" Without missing a beat Little Portia said "I want a Purple Mommy!" It wasn't deep (She was 5 at the time) but it was fun. It was playful and silly and clear: I could be any sort of mommy as long as I was purple! As long as I did not grow up.

I drafted a notepad manifesto of what a "Purple Mommy" was and have used it as a touchstone in my parenting. There are statements like "Encourage Laughter" and "Simple housekeeping" along with deeper thoughts of "Live towards God" and what became our family motto "Live Well". My kids remind me when I slide away from being a purple mommy. Having them around makes me very aware of how I am living my life.

As they grew older and resisted correction and consequences I told them the Secret of Adulthood: All adults want to have fun all the time. Since parents are the rule guardians, kids need to know we actually prefer to have fun. The better behaved everyone is, the more energy we have for all the fun.

At work it is different. Even at a church we are cubicles and offices, staplers and business cards. There are meetings, some are boring. We recently had a staff leadership retreat and during one break, stiff and tired as I was, I decided to challenge my colleagues to a youthful game of tag. Let me be clear I am not a 'run about' sort of woman. I don't do sporty, so suggesting a game of tag with a room full of grownups was quite a reach for me personally. I wanted all of us to shake off the weariness and have a bit of play. No one else wanted that. Not a single person played tag with me. I felt kind of stupid, BUT it was good for me to risk looking foolish. I never want to take myself too seriously. It was good for me to at least consider moving faster than a saunter, even if only in a single burst of play.

I don't always dress my age, either. I mean, I'm not displaying my belly button ring or anything, but I have some fun. I color the underside of my normal hair teal and purple in the modern mullet of hair color. I try wild prints and tulle princess skirts that make me smile. Lula Roe clothes have brought me out of my all black Chicago fashion style into happy prints and drapey fabric that make play and adventure possible.

I play with my words. I am quick to make a joke. I did not get mad when my kids upended a bag of glitter in my car to make me laugh... and I left it there for months. We purchased silly string to bomb a friend's yard...haven't used it, but knowing it is there makes me feel younger.

My husband and I watched Mark Marron's comedy bit where he says "I don't know how long I've got...." to get out of things he doesn't want to waste his time doing. We love and use that sentence often because none of us knows how long we have. We don't have to act our age. We can play even if we are grown up adults.

Even if people scowl at our youthful antics, we'll know that we are showing them a better way. Their brain just needs time to catch up. Let's not stop our play to wait for them. Remember, we were old once, too.

GRANDMOTHER KNEW

Long ago my Grandmother Lutes said I should be a writer. I'll bet some of you have a grandma who said you would be a great writer, too. It is a typical beloved family member thing to say. I wrote letters by hand in those days (Yup, I am that old). After the dinosaurs died out and we enjoyed the industrial age, I wrote a typed missive of a Christmas Letter to send to everyone including Grandma. I was funny and pithy and challenged them to live better lives. Soon I was writing training courses for my job, and marketing copy and sales scripts. While I do not think any of that would make Grandma proud like my letters to her, I had fun with the words no matter their purpose.

I continued to write, mostly in journals and a few hopeful pieces crafted for NPR radio. (Crafted, not sent.) Once I wrote a piece with fire in my soul and tears on my cheeks and sent it to our own April Lidinsky. Would she like it? Was it not just 'good enough for Grandma'? April did like it! She asked if I wanted to read it on the radio and yes oh yes oh yes I did! That went well enough. They invited me to keep doing it and I have inflicted my chatty ruminations upon all of you for ten years now. I later wrote for my own blog and several others. I kept a journal, over posted my witticisms on social media and pretended to write a book.

One day I took a trip to Sierra Leone, West Africa. I shared about that in another Michiana Chronicle, if you missed it. I went equipped with three journals. I knew I'd get some great stories from my wild adventure. While I was prepared logistically for the trip, I was never prepared emotionally for the firsthand experience of a developing country. I lost my writer's voice. My journals were empty and all I could do was scratch out a haiku here and there. If you are unfamiliar, a haiku is a Japanese form poem consisting of three lines, 5 syllables in the first line, 7 syllables in the second line and five syllables again in the third line. My Dad writes hundreds of them. Friends and I have played back and forth with haiku. I have written many little poems.   In Africa, haikus were all I could write. The rigid format was the only way I could distill all the emotions and experiences of my first world travel. I wrote 54 haiku over my two weeks there.

Once home from my trip, I was invited to speak several times about the trip and what I learned. I shared my writer's block, photographs and a few haiku. My beloved Aunt Ruth and Uncle Frank watched a video of my talk online and contacted me. They wanted to donate to Operation Classroom, as I requested during the talk. I want to raise $3,000 for the Taiama Enterprise Academy, AKA The TEA, I visited in Sierra Leone. As we talked, my Aunt Ruth shared her conviction that many people would enjoy the story and the lessons I pulled from my trip. She thought the haiku were unique and the photos were gripping. She asked me, "Have you considered putting them together into a book?" She said creating a book could make a long-term revenue stream for Operation Classroom, and thus for the TEA. My heart raced and I stood taller with pride. We continued to dream together.

I started out researching photo book pricing, then self publishing, and submitted the concept to a few places. I angsted over paying $350 or more to have it formatted, then realized I used Canva and could format the book myself! I ignored my poor family as I hunched over the computer to work. I sweated, swore and cried over edit after edit. I hate an unfinished project and since the haiku were written and the photos were snapped, it was just a matter of placement. I visited printers, learned about perfect binding, offset presses and how many companies want to charge A LOT of extra money if you need any help at all. I deftly sidestepped it all. I read articles and stalked my author friends. I tried to decide if I was embarrassed to self publish or thrilled because I would get more profits to turn over to Operation Classroom. I ordered author proofs, stalked the UPS truck and at last held my book in my lap with tears in my eyes. I had a real live book with an ISBN and book signings were lined up!

Writing a book will never be this easy; this was divinely inspired and familial-ly financed. (It is worth mentioning that Uncle Frank is one of my mother's dear brothers, son of that Grandmother who thought I should be a writer.) I don't know how well it will sell beyond the initial print run of several hundred copies. I'm not sure if my Grandmother was right, or if people even like haiku or if they are too busy to care about a school in a remote village on another continent. I am proud of these pages and I think my Grandma would be too.

NEW HERE

It is not even 8:30 in the morning when she has stormed upstairs and I have slammed a door and bellowed that our fun plans for the day are canceled. I sit in the bathroom where I am hiding from her, fuming. I am too mad to pray. I'm too mad to write. I'm too mad to think in any kind of a reasonable straight line.

She is eight years old, and usually the kindest, most helpful child. This morning she is attempting a sewing project without help or guidance. It involves a pattern and tracing paper and again, she is only eight years old. I didn't mind helping her, but my kind of help is adulting. I want to teach and demonstrate The Right Way To Do It. I know she is frustrated with her littleness. I know like every crafter on the planet, her vision is perfection and her reality is whatever she is able to do right now in this space with her own little learning hands.

I still lost my cool. I got angry and yelled at her when she yelled at me. Instead of absorbing her feelings for her and loving her though them, I retaliated with my feelings. I am a grown ass woman, fighting with a precious innocent eight year old. I am then also mad at myself. Why on earth would I be such a reactive jerk to this person I adore? Why at my age and wisdom do I sink to the ground to an eight year old's emotional level and just react? I settled down and was able to pray and then I got it: No one else in my life treats me like this, and if they did they would not be in my life.

I am not about to break up with my beloved daughter, but it was a helpful realization that our children treat us worse than anyone else we allow in our lives. We are supposed to be a safe place for them to lose it...yet most of us fail to stay zen when a person, however small, is spewing vitriol in our direction. We are hurt! We are offended! We want to stop the flow of negative emotions quickly. But...we are parents, too. Do any of you have tips to help the rest of us not melt down when they do?

My husband and I have a mantra we use at times like this: "They are new here." Reminding ourselves the kids are new here to the planet, to the world, helps us remember they do not know what we know. The things that are obvious to us are not obvious to them and we need to allow them room to discover some truths on their own. My expectations are high and I do not apologize for that. I can still teach to their level and remain a reasonable adult at the same time. Right?

Our kids are independent and mostly awesome. They help with chores big and small, dress themselves, run the neighborhood unsupervised and have learned to clean up their own messes literally and figuratively. As I wrote this, Libby came to me with tear stained cheeks and apologized for yelling at me. She then asked me how she could make it up to me. She is eight years old but knows how to clean up the inevitable mess of relationships better than many adults. I told her I was sorry too, and that I was writing about our struggle. I said that if she would let me share it with you guys, it would help me a lot. She agreed. We cuddled and talked about what went wrong with her doll sewing pattern and I offered a trip to the craft store for better tools.

It may help you to know that remembering a person is "New Here" may work in most any situation. Each of us are new here; new to this day, that job, this difficult negotiation of feelings. Perhaps remember we ourselves are 'new here'... new to this very moment. We all carry our experience of the world with us into every new interaction. Each hour of our days is different from the last. I give you these two little words to remember to care gently for yourself, your children, friends, family and strangers....we are all new here, after all.

ADVENTURE IS OUT THERE

So I took a trip this Fall. I have ventured all over the United States and also went to Cancun as is required for most young people mid winter. Once, when I was way up north in Michigan for a work assignment, I ventured over the bridge to a Canadian Tim Hortons. Then I went back across the bridge because it was late and I was tired. I never had a passport. I suck at geography. Even as lovely church missionaries and Doctors without Borders and Peace Corps people head across the ocean to help other people in other countries, I was content here at home in Indiana.

One day, the heavens and stars aligned to send me on the trip of a lifetime and I said: "No Thanks!" My church's international mission team wanted to pay for someone, maybe someone like me, to go to Sierra Leone, West Africa with Operation Classroom. I said "No thanks". The price tag on such a trip was over $3,000 for those of you keeping track at home. I could go for free. I suggested ten other souls much more likely to agree and better equipped than me for such an undertaking. I told my dear husband that maybe just maybe, if everyone else said "no", I would consider the trip. My dear husband, considering being left alone with our household and children for two weeks, simply said, "Well, you'd need a passport."

I slowly realized I wasn't getting out of this. I understood at last I needed to go on this trip to break out of the rut of middle-aged parenthood and its trappings. I finally said "yes". I started buying all the things an entitled American could need to go to a humid, sweltering, mosquito ridden African country. I got that passport. I got a yellow fever shot and a mosquito net. I wrote out childcare directions for friends who love me enough to read and mostly follow them. I changed our wills.

Preparing for this trip did nothing to prepare me for this trip. Our trip coordinator had extensive details and suggestions and caveats that kept all the basics aligned, but you guys! The world! The world is out there! I have always espoused the need to shake up routines; in our minds, our traveled paths to work and the grocery store, the stories we tell ourselves. Traveling to another continent, living in another country amidst a different culture changed me to the core. Traveling changes you, too. The world! The world is out there and adventure awaits!

The purpose of the trip with Operation Classroom was to celebrate and support the grand opening of the first STEM school in Sierra Leone. The school was part of a refurbished secondary school in the village of Taiama, Sierra Leone. I went with five other people, three of whom I already knew; the other two would become new friends. I thought we would help the people there. I don't know that I helped much at all but I learned. I learned that African Time is a thing, in which the American punctuality is non-existent and meetings may start hours after the suggested start time. I learned that people in poverty, washing dishes on the dirt ground or playing with literal trash are happier than most Americans I know... including myself. The village where no one has 'anything', as far as my self-centered yardstick could tell, that village had more life in it than many of our American neighborhoods.   The African sense of relationship, community, peace and joy was the biggest surprise to me on the trip. The students at the Taiama school and the Taiama Enterprise Academy(also called The TEA) really want to be in school. Their desire for knowledge and their respect for education eclipsed every child I know. Even my own children.

Traveling to another part of the world taught me (in the way a book or news story never could) how much we are all alike. Travelling taught me the true value of all that I have. I am also learning the richness of intangible things. Meeting children my own children may never meet, living lives my daughters could not imagine has reshaped my mamahood. I am better and wiser after going on this mission trip I didn't want to take. Is there a trip you need to take? There are cheap ways to tour places around the world. There are a bajillion blogs sharing tips to save money and go adventure on the cheap. There are mission trips saving you a spot. The world is out there, have you been?

TECH RAGE

You know how your parents or grandparents are too...old...to understand technology? How can you explain it slowly, simply but still no comprende? They cannot learn this crucial technology fast enough, and they need your help all the time. Technology matters to our daily lives. (Especially under quarantine lockdown where the only thing between most of us and a complete psychotic break is a little glowing screen.) I know not all of the boomer-plus set are lost when it comes to tech...many folks are savvy. My family runs the gamut from "Me Text You Long Time" with texts so long they should be an email to "Won't Get a Facebook Page" even if they could see their grandkids' daily life through that lens. I have a love hate relationship with technology myself, mostly because I am stupid.

While I do have a college degree and some lovely certifications, when it comes to technology, my brain reacts much in the same way it does to mathematics: "No Thanks". It is a firm and swift "No Thank You", curt and ungracious. While on the outside I appear a capable adult, on the inside I struggle with remembering the password

I use on this site or that. I can manage people, a speaking business, continuing education, a church volunteer team and my family life...but I cannot log into my Canva account on the first try. Ever.

When this whole lockdown for the Corona Virus began, I was awesome. I set up a Zoom account without ever having used it before! I did this so my nine-year-old could have an online quarantine playdate with her friend. I created the meeting, sent the invite to my friend Becca and waited for the magic to start. Half an hour later when the playdate zoom meeting was to begin, I couldn't log back in! My friend was texting to see where I was, her daughter had logged into the meeting and was ready and waiting. As I fervently attempted to log my kid in, my blood pressure skyrocketed. After several poor attempts to sign on to the meeting I had created, we handed over our phones so they could just use our FB messenger chat. UGH.

I try to get a lot of weird work done in little pockets of opportunity. I work part time for a church, and I also have a public speaking business. I am motivated and work best within my own flow, cramming days of work into a few focused, diligent hours...and nothing in between. (Nothing being family life, daily household care and before Covid-19, a social life!) When I'm creating marketing pieces and social media images and scheduling posts in Later.com I am creative, lively and competent. I love encouraging others to live well. Unfortunately, my dirty secret is it may take me up to an hour to get started once I sit at a computer, laptop or iPad. FORGOT PASSWORD leads to RESET PASSWORD and then which of my four emails did I use? Was it my professional password style or personal? Old one or newest one after I forgot the last time?

I wear myself out just getting ready to work with technology. Am I really just simple minded, or can some of you relate to this tech intelligence breach too? I think the solution could be using that ever popular Password1234 as my universal password. Maybe I need to throw an ampersand in there to honor the password request for a Capital letter, number, and symbol. I know the hackers could get into my accounts that way.... but maybe after they breach my checking account, they could tell me how to get in too?

I know these are great problems to have in the scope of life. I am also certain there are better solutions than throwing my device across the room or banging on it like an elevator door button, but I am not that mature yet. My husband tries to help me, based on his love for his wife, his desire to not have me break something and also a bit of fear at how loud I can yell at an unresponsive iPad. I love him for trying.

I hope to get better with age, with maturity. I'm not holding my breath, but I am holding hope. I love what I can do with tech when we get along, and I do not want to give up yet. Just don't tell my husband I threw the laptop on the ground in frustration from another tech induced rage. I told him the kids broke it. They are the only ones smart enough to use it in the first place.

NAILED IT!

Unless you live under the proverbial rock, what I am about to say should spark recognition: "Nailed it!!" Do you know it? This current standard in our 'Pinworthy' YouTube Social Media World should make you cringe or smile. "Nailed it!" is the recognition that what we see, what we attempt, and what we actually create...do not match. (Google the phrase when you need a belly laugh.) If you were a gymnast, "nailing it" would indicate mastery and perfection. Shall we imagine together that it originated in carpentry? "Nailing it" would be pretty direct and to the point! For our purposes today we are taking the pop culture definition of "Nailed it!" to mean, in truth we have failed it.

In our house we struggle to find cinematic entertainment we all agree on. One likes Sci fi, one likes adventure, one likes mermaids and I like books. We stumbled onto the Netflix show "Nailed It!" and all four of us were riveted. If you haven't heard of it, three obviously unskilled bakers attempt to recreate clever, artistic, intricate baked goods. They create ornate, sculpted cakes, famous people made out of Eclairs or some such craziness.

Each contestant runs to pick their project and the hosts are funny and dramatically loud. We love it. We laugh and we watch together.

Last year we challenged friends and neighbors to join us on a Unicorn Cake "Nailed it!" from the comfort of their own homes. My entire family got into crafting multi colored cake layers, creating and shaping unicorn features from fondant (a baker's edible playdoh) and sugar glitter. It was a gorgeous disaster. If you ever wonder why a bakery charges $50 for a Unicorn Cake, you try making one and then gleefully fork out that cash!

This summer as we stayed home and looked for ways to pass the time, I brought books home from the library. Our library offers curb side so I could browse and request online and pick up outside! We got The Food Network's <u>Big, Fun Kids Cookbook</u> and began paging through it. I told the girls they could each pick something (ANYTHING!) out and we would make it. No surprise they both picked "Fake Out" cakes. Portia picked a Macaroni and Cheese Cake. Libby chose an Ice Cream Cake shaped to look like a Strawberry Crunch Ice Cream Bar. I looked over the ingredient lists and it was pretty straightforward: frosting, cake mix, ice cream, debris.

The first attempt was the mac and cheese cake. I basically stayed out of the kitchen and the girls went wild. They mixed the white chocolate melting wafers with food coloring and piped them out onto waxed paper to make the noodles. The cake is baked in a bowl to make the shape of a bowl. As we searched for a container that could take the heat of the oven, Portia gleefully discovered my vintage Pyrex was oven safe! The result had them laughing and eating in equal amounts of delight. They "Nailed it!".

Portia was otherwise occupied the day we made Libby's cake. I stepped in as an assistant. I was a poor assistant. First, I left our downstairs freezer unplugged for two days. The food was fine, but the ice cream needed for the middle of the cake was very unfrozen. The excess cake cuts and freeze dried strawberries came together well for the coating, but everything else was a comedy, or a tragedy. Libby did her parts well, as for me...I nailed it. It was hard! The ice cream was soggy! The cake fell apart when I cut the sheet cake in half horizontally. I resolved that by flipping the damaged side to the bottom and slathering everything else with more frosting. It was delicious.

Giving the girls projects to tackle (and then eat!) was a great adventure. The book had all sorts of mostly kid friendly recipes and we may go after another one soon. All of us learned grace, and patience and that ugliness can taste pretty good if you add sugar. We saw first-hand that what looks so simple may not quite turn out, but a positive attitude and deep breaths get us through it. The lessons learned in our kitchen this summer can be applied to life at large; when we 'fail it', we can work together to fix what is broken, soggy and ruined. We can support each other and try something new. No matter what tears, disasters and clean up awaits, at the end of the day we can get out our forks and claim "Nailed it!" together.

ROLL 20

What in the world is going on in the world? Without reducing the gravity of the really important, painful truths we are working on together, may I invite you to step aside into escapist delights? Let your mind wander, close your eyes if you aren't driving and step into the woods. As you walk along the sun dappled path, leaves crunch under your feet and the smell of damp earth fills your nostrils. Birds twitter and a squirrel runs across the path. Your senses tighten within the idyllic moment and you pause. You release your canteen and survey the path ahead seeing nothing. You unscrew the copper lid from the wine skin and tip it to your lips filling your mouth with coppery, metallic tasting liquid. You cap the bag and as you return it to your belt you hear them. In the bushes up to the right there is a snort, a jingle from armor and you wave your hand for your party to stop. You draw your bow and arrow knowing it is likely an Orc patrol. You should be able to dispatch them easily. You are a fighter, the woman behind you a sorceress, the two dwarves behind her have been spoiling for an encounter. The Elven Cleric will pray, and fight, and afterwards heal any wounds around the campfire or at the ubiquitous inn where it all begins.

I am a perfectly normal, well mostly normal woman of a certain age, and for the first time in my life, I play Dungeons and Dragons. It started when our tween daughter Portia spent more time in her room reading about dragons and warrior cats, and less with us. We wanted a way to connect, to play together as she grew older and away from us. I bought the Essentials and Beginners Kits as Christmas gifts for my husband. I was clueless about the game and wanted to have everything we could need to start. I bought beautiful pewter figures from The Griffon in downtown South Bend. I chose a pretty woman in a dress, someone with a bow pulled taut, a big guy in armor with a sword and a person with a walking stick and a tiger. I had to have lots of help picking them out. I now know they are a Sorceress or Cleric, a Ranger, a Fighter and a Druid. I have learned a lot of things since Christmas 2019!

At first we just read everything over and over. I posted the words "Dungeons & Dragons?" On my Facebook page, too embarrassed to elaborate. I only played one time in high school, but I knew playing admitted some things I wasn't ready to say out loud. I'd hoped someone who played would respond and draw us in...and they did. Michael and Marci embraced our spindly, tentative steps into D&D with the Mines of Phandelver adventure in the Beginners Kit. Now my husband is "DM" (Dungeon Master) for "The Dragon of Icespire Peak" adventure. He draws out maps for the figures, offers us lego structures for visual perspective in combat, and fights with me. We have disagreed several times about whether Vani Greenbottle, my Halfling Rogue character, has an athletics check high enough to climb the pole out of a pit. SPOILER: She doesn't. Part of the fun in the game is that when you want to do something, you often have to roll a 20 sided dice to see if you will be successful. The DM will decide and often tell colorful interpretations of what happened with your effort. Roll 20 affects actions, combat and also your character's ability to avoid harm, sense trouble or discover secrets along the way.

I've since learned that many fine folks play D&D. They aren't the 40 year olds living with their parents of legend. They are professionals who need to escape for a few hours. Parents want to grow and learn with their kids. Older people rekindle their love for storytelling. D&D is showing up in TV and movies and have you watched Critical Role? Both of our daughters play and add such nuances to each character that playing together is a highlight of my week. We have bought more books and delved deeper into worlds away from our own. We have bought multiple pretty dice sets...for some reason you always want more. #DiceDragon We have several dozen figurines, some pewter, some painted plastic. They sit on the door frame of our dining room so we can enjoy this new adventure all week.

Our real world is hard right now. It is filled with giants and dragons and evil that seems overwhelming. Do the hard things first, and then allow yourself a break. Head to a game store. They will help connect you to a game or get you the supplies needed to escape for a few hours. Sit down to a D&D game, close your eyes and travel to the forest...we could use your help battling these Orcs!

THE LIGHT OF THE WORLD

It is so very cold, and it is so very dark. The cold seeps into my bones and makes me want to just sit here in my chair with a fuzzy blanket and slippers. I only have energy to zone out in a book or watch Netflix until my eyes dry out. We accidentally ate dinner at four o'clock because it was so dark and we were so dull we didn't realize it was not evening. Even in this winter chill, there is a kindling warmth. Under the dark, there is a spark of light, a glimmer of hope. In the world where we may feel battered and bruised and disappointed and afraid, there is a small light cast into this day by a tiny baby in a manger.

Oh, I know it might not be a tiny baby for you. Call it eight nights of light when there should have only been one. Maybe you set that Yule Log on fire and hang an upside down tree. Call it that one day we all overindulge and give each other gifts we do not need but deeply enjoy. That day where we ask ourselves to suspend adult pragmatism and tell stories to children of a fat man with reindeer and a sleigh full of hopes and dreams shaped as candy and toys. I hope we can love each other enough it won't matter what we call it. My single prayer this Christmas Day is that we can love one another enough to spread the light.

Humanity tells itself stories to help us learn things better. There are many religions in the world and there is the absence of religion and there are writers and prayers and ordinary people reaching out with their own words. It is easy to hear stories we recognize, as it is easy to love our beloved ones. It is harder to listen with our whole souls to other stories. It is hard to think of that person we disagree with as someone's Father or Son or Holy Baby. I tell my daughters to live life with an "open hand". It usually comes up when they are fighting over some toy or piece of clothing. I just say, "Open Hand...." Which means do not hold too tightly to anything because you cannot share good things that way. If we live with a tightly closed hand, we also cannot fully receive good things from others. We want to keep what matters from being taken away by other people. We feel safe drawing a line between ours and theirs and yet we all trip over the line. We get hurt by it. We hurt others with the line.

The small spark of hope, light, warmth, love...it belongs to you. It belongs to each of us when we listen to the Other story. The light belongs to us when we ask ourselves, "What is true here?" or "Could I be mistaken?" When we smile at strangers or harried, overwhelmed cashiers... the light is ours. When we lay down on the floor next to our tantrum-ing child, the child rude and angry, but we lay beside them to show them we are for them. We are offering a spark of light to them. When we stand up for someone being hurt or disrespected, we offer our light to them and it grows larger.

When my day is lousy for whatever reasons, reaching out to encourage someone (anyone)else never fails to lift my spirits. My light, my love grows and multiplies when I make the effort to share it. Even in dark, cold days like we have seen. We owe it to ourselves and each other to offer this light to everyone around us even if just for self-preservation!

Maybe this cold, dark, weariness is seasonal. Maybe it is political. Maybe it is pandemical...??? Each of us has the same feelings with different names. Whatever words we use, we must hold fast to the belief that there will be light and warmth and love. This active, vibrant spark is what hope looks like. There is hope for you, hope for me and there is hope for them. We each hold the spark to bring the light of hope and a better tomorrow. It doesn't matter how you celebrate today. Hope is born anew every single day. It is up to you and I to celebrate the light of hope with others.

Merry Christmas. May we be like the light of

the world.

INTERESTED?

The thing I want all of you to know is there was one time I nailed this stay at home mama deal. Sure, it was just that once, but since I left my job in August, I am here for the small wins! One day the house was kind of tidy, the kids got haircuts, we researched the past owners of our hundred year old house and I voted. I also laid out a tray of hot cocoa and fresh oil popped popcorn for a pal and her brood. It was a socially-distanced-bonfire-and-whatever-you-find-in-the-garage playdate. Then I put dinner on the table. I kind of impressed myself. This ONE day. Feeling accomplished around here is a rare occurrence.

The part that meant the most to me was the voting. I had lots of feelings taking my girls with me to vote. I believe it is important and every person should do it. I told the girls it was a right, a privilege AND a responsibility to vote in every election they can. I worried as I talked (AGAIN) to my young daughters about the importance of voting and (AGAIN) about the hard fought battle for our votes as women they tuned me out. (When I read this to them, Libby vehemently stated she did not tune me out!) They do get feisty over politics, fed as they are by our loud, opinionated (and yet fact based!) adult conversations. I have brought my kids to prayer vigils, to protests, and to courthouses with handmade signs. I want them to be interesting people. I want them to be INTERESTED people.

When I speak at mom conferences, I often share a story about what my Dad said to me as a new wife and mother. I was fumbling through the bleary days of cloth diapers and tiny humans when my Dad asked, "Are you keeping yourself fresh for your husband?" (Uhhh, what?!?) As I picked my jaw up off the floor, he clarified. He was asking if I was interesting. He wasn't talking about lady bits, he meant was I more than the sum of motherhood? (AHHHH. Yes!) It was one of the most powerful questions in my life and that is why I share the embarrassing truth with you. The question asks, "Am I interested in the world beyond my own house and family? Do I make an effort to learn new things? Do I read the paper, go to weird places, help my neighbors? Am I interesting to speak with when my husband comes home? Do I take care of my brain as a person?"

This question fueled my life and motherhood ever since. Last week the girls remarked they know what they eat at dinner is rarely traditional kid food. They are both pescatarian while John and I still eat meat. We are proud of their choice and cook vegetarian food at home. We say yes to new adventures and leatherworking and hot glue and learning experiences. The kids have attended Dr. Martin Luther King Day conferences at the local University, we geocache, and explore the world around us. We once again take the PAPER Paper so the kids can see current events on their own. I read poetry and books I would not naturally gravitate to, simply to expand my little hamster wheel mind. I traveled to Sierra Leone & wrote a book. I try to ask good questions in conversation. I have finally learned other people have more to say than will come out in surface conversation. It takes work to shove my family off the couch and walk the dog in a new wild place, but that work keeps things interesting. It keeps us interesting.

The fastest way for me to improve my life is to do something new. Movement is what creates change in our souls. Consider today what new experience you want to undertake? While our respective adventures may not interest everyone, we are all interesting. In this season of staying home with my kids, my focus is creating a thirst for interest in them. I want them to invest themselves in other people, to learn about the world outside their circle and to pursue what makes them sparkle.   What do you know that the rest of us could enjoy and grow from? What area of learning could you research or borrow or immerse yourselves in? Are you keeping yourself fresh for us? Whatever your days look like, remember this: An interested person leads an interesting life.

JUST STUCK

I got to play in the snow this week. We got nineteen inches give or take eighty. So I played in the snow but not in a fun way. I played in 'the dog won't go on her own and you don't want her to pee on the porch" sort of way. Our poor sedan that should be put out to pasture got stuck TWICE in one day. I told my husband John to just leave it there with a 'FREE PLEASE TAKE' sign.

Like the car, I also got stuck in a snowdrift. I'd run out without a coat or gloves to move our car a few feet away from the shoveled sidewalk. I tried to slip around the end of the car but with the fabulous nineteen inches, I tumbled off kilter into the piled snow. I was stuck... half in half out of a three-foot drift. I was kneeling in several feet of snow but couldn't stand up. There was nothing to grab on to. I had to put my bare hands into the snow, the rough ice crystals jabbing against my hands and face. The powder of it meant I just sank. It was like swimming in your freezer. I struggled to move my toasty warm but heavy booted feet. I kicked and flailed and finally rolled over on my back and half crawled, half rolled into the street. I felt so ungainly it was like being nine months pregnant all over again. No, it was like being pregnant and trying to roll over in bed. If my sheets and nightgown were both flannel. And if my bed were in the middle of the street. There was definitely swearing as at last I stood anything but victorious and covered in snow.

Our kids have enjoyed actually playing in the snow. This joy is increased as it is the only safe way our family is social these days. The kids are remote learning and just had a winter break followed by an actual snow day followed by an eLearning day. As if the past YEAR of familial togetherness wasn't enough, we got …. more time. Together at home. Just the four of us. More time together. I have been more irritable and so is everyone else. I know I am not alone in loosening our pandemic restrictions…I'm not the only one trying to get strangers driving by the house to take one of the kids for the weekend. I spent two hours locked in my bedroom last weekend just to be alone and my sweet husband got nervous. Whether he was nervous I would leave him or leave him with the kids I do not know….but I told him he had nothing to worry about. Those children though…

I'm kidding. I'm pretty much kidding? I shouldn't whine and complain because I know I'm experiencing an A+ Pandemic experience. We have steady income, we are healthy and we like each other. Our extended family is all on the same page with precautions and social distancing so there is no strife. And we have money in our budget for weekly restaurant delivery...thus the Covid 19 "Nineteen" I am working on. I'm not there quite yet...who knows? Who cares? We are at the stage when we are weary from 2021 and it has barely started. Alcohol is important. Copious snacking options are important. Good things to read from the library and all the Internet subscriptions are a priority. We finally saved up enough to buy a new couch since it is a literal lifeboat each day. And we are also getting a bigger chair with room for both of my girls to snuggle up with me. For more togetherness.

My basement has been kinda purged and my house is kinda clean and the laundry is still in piles so that isn't new. The Holderness Family parodies and random TikTok videos make me howl with laughter and remember that we are all so alike. We keep finding fun things to do. We are doing a Netflix "Nailed It! at Home" baking event this weekend, and I think we might also try making snow ice cream. Hey! At least then the next time I'm trapped in a mini avalanche snowbank, I could maybe eat my way out to safety.

ROYALTY

Friends, I have a confession to make: I am not just your average stay at home mama. I am a little famous. Nobody knows I am famous. Well, my kids do. I feel like a million bucks anytime they say "Mom! You are famous!" This exclamation is usually in response to a stranger knowing me through speaking, my book, NPR radio, the internet or commercials. Or if they Google me. (Guys, we should never Google ourselves, and our kids should DEFINITELY not Google us. YIKES.) I've always been a force and I love an audience of any size. My husband, John, introduces himself in some circles as "Heather's Husband" since that will inevitably be his initial moniker anyway.

John recently expressed some concern about his historical social standing compared to mine. I know I married 'up' , so I do not understand this. Maybe it is my father's mother Portia's mother (also named Portia) who published a book about her wild life? The book tells her story from South Carolina to Russia to Sterling, Colorado. It includes the family Huguenot lineage, Portia becoming a Doctor in South Carolina, and her husband Alexis Lubchenco missing a cruise aboard Titanic.

There's also the tale that Alexander Kerensky helped them escape Moscow when the Russian revolution began. And he also greeted Big Mama Portia by name in a South Carolina elevator when she greeted him in Russian. Fascinating.

Then there is my Mother's side of things. During our summer vacation to Colorado, John got a glimpse of the other half of my family history. This took shape in the form of a gorgeous wood and glass display case in my Uncle Frank's home. My Aunt Ruth shared the stories of the items displayed. She spoke of Senators, the Teller brothers who built the Teller House in Central City, Colorado and the Victorian French Fragrance bottle from Paris that was a gift from someone important. I remember the intricate bottle living under a plexiglass case on a fancy marble stand sitting in my grandparent's home.

As I look down the barrel of a milestone birthday, I find my roots utterly fascinating. Family history wasn't very interesting when I was younger. I thought I was interesting. As an only child growing up in some hard situations, I learned to talk to adults instead of my peers. I wanted to be noticed, to stay up with the adults, to be adored.

I was obnoxious.

I know I was trying to earn my right to be present by being funny, cute and talented.

This led to high school and community plays. It launched an acting career I guess I've never left. After some extras work in films, local and national commercials (that "Every Woman" Oprah commercial, I'm in that!) I moved on. I did dramas for a mega church with 5,000 attending each Sunday. Seeing my face on TV and screen made me feel good. Great, actually. I later used my acting skills in sales, training folks to sell and teaching customer service. My friend Jenny kept me honest as I pursued acting in Chicago. She said, "Just because you act like a movie star, doesn't mean you are one"!

I would humblebrag more here, but I have something better. In pursuit of worth and star status, I literally became royalty. Last year I learned about Noble Society Services where as a gift you can buy a share of land with a title. I asked my husband if he wanted a Scottish Laird Title for Christmas and he declined. But. My Dad didn't need anything for Christmas, and Groupon had a deep discount, so he became the Tsar of Marinovka. Marinovka is a teeny little forest in Zirgan, Republic of Bashkortostan (Near the Village of Nordovka, which is near Allaguvat, a more rural village with only three streets and population of 154 people). We received GPS coordinates and two beautiful documents; one in English, the other in Russian. My Father, James Alexis Curlee is now a Tsar. Which means I am a princess. Somewhat legit. I paid an extra five bucks each for my daughters and I to get similar title paperwork for ourselves. According to Nobility Services, we can officially use our Groupon priced Royalty for our legal documents and getting a good table at a restaurant. You may kiss the ring, and can we please have a window seat?

My edges have softened with time, and I know I have worth even without an audience. I listen better and talk less, finding other people's stories more interesting than my own. While I remain a little famous (and a Russian Princess), my current family keeps me grounded. I do not have housekeeping staff and the paparazzi attention has fallen off in recent years. In the words of my Peter Mayer theme song, "Nobody knows I'm famous, so I have to go around and say it."

PANTY RAID

May I speak with you of scanties? Really
'panties' is what I meant to say,

I've judged them harshly (and the women
in them) in almost every way

In my twenties all my panties had to
match my bras in color or tone

And if the laundry languished undone,

I would simply wear none!

The mamas I knew wore ratty tatty briefs

and it made me lecture On their sex-ure

as I begged them to wear something with texture

A bit of lace, a strip of slinky satin,
anything luscious

It pained my soul for them to be deprived
of Goddess level touches!

Called 'thunder thighs' as an
adolescent, I wanted to be lean

But God made me curvy so that's what I've been!

I love to dress myself well from bottom to top

And even when older that would never stop.

So I dressed for romance and scandals

and caressed my beloved love handles

Even when it was just me and my kitties

My pretty bra always matched my panties

I had beautiful daughters and
happy marriage feats

Lost that monthly guest and enjoyed more treats

As happiness fed me in all of the ways

My personality and girth

increased with the days

Remember my panties?

My sexpot platform on undies?

I kept it up (mostly) through nursing
and decades of fun days

But as my flesh swelled, eventually
I considered taking the leap

To tucking myself into some big comfy briefs

Would I die as a sexual creature in bigger knickers?

Was it giving up, ignoring my
younger self's snickers?

As I stretched out my bikini underwear over time

I tried one pair of brief panties

which were completely sublime!

Briefs tucked in (and welcomed!)
my dismaying belly roll

They smoothed me and held me
until they were full.

I was immediately torn between sexy and comfort

So I did the math and at my age I
could keep this secret covert

I tossed the stretched out symbols of youth

Bought more briefs in all colors
and textures (Truth!)

With my bits tucked in and my flaps smoothed out

I felt sexier than ever and knew
what it was all about

Life gives us sex and children and food

But we each get to choose our daily mood

feeling sexy or comfy it is all up to us

At any age we can choose without all the fuss

I want to be kind to my body and love myself

Even without little panties, now on the shelf

My value, joy and love comes
from the life that I live

Each new day offers more than a
thong could ever give.

MEME IS ME

We all want to be special and unique. This is the force behind advertising that promises a better 'us' in one product and three clicks. Our need to be wonderful moves us to post snaps of our dinner, our feet and our dogs for social media. Carefully curated online lives help us to show only our best self, only in the best light. We post pictures and witty words to show we are unique like everyone else in our feed. I used to chortle up my sleeve in high school at the rebellious kids wearing black lipstick and mohawks to be unique...like the rest of their friends. I didn't care much about fashion beyond what made me happy in my budget. I was neither popular nor shunned. Those days of my youth are long past and today my desires are the same. I don't make 'Duck lips' in photos anymore, but I want to be seen and noticed. I want to be special. Today my desire to be special makes me so much like the people around me, I have become a meme and the meme is me. Ermahgerd!

I am a startlingly clear sample of a middle-aged white lady target customer. I am typical and predictable even as I strive to be unique. I first realized this on my honeymoon fifteen years ago.

I was on a plane with my tray table down and a Good Housekeeping magazine spread wide open. As a new bride, I was drawn to the vision of perfect domesticity offered within the pages. I grinned to see the very jeans I wore there on the page in an advertisement. There was another article with recipes I would make while on the same honeymoon. I felt like Good Housekeeping was written just for me.

Lately I am the Insurance ads about "How Not to Become Your Parents". I'd guess they target millennials, because my Gen X self is exactly who they make fun of. My husband gives me a hard side eye when they come on and say, "The waiter doesn't need to know your name." I make one-hour friends with staff everywhere. I hope it validates their hard work and I feel kinder...but... well. When I wore my Gap sweatshirt "Live Love Laugh", I saw myself as the woman in the "How Not to Become Your Parents" ad tossing away a similar wooden sign.

My social media feeds are crammed with boozy, funny women sharing the same six memes every week. Memes about being hideously marginal parents, sculpting free time to read behind a locked bathroom door or cussing. I follow so many people that are so alike and share the same memes that I have begun unfollowing almost everyone to get a break. Heck yes the one that goes "Parenting is wandering around everyday whispering WTF to yourself(OH wait, we are supposed to whisper that?)." is hilarious. It is 100% relevant to me, but I see it a few times a week because I am a predictable demographic. I am not unique.

My husband and I laugh together almost daily at some brief joke on the internet that jabs at our lives. We love videos like The Holderness Family parody "Me at 20 vs. Me at 40". The jokes are so spot on they have been viewed more than two hundred million jillion times. Many of us at my stage in life see ourselves reflected in Holderness Family comedy. Like them and their audience, I've tried and failed with cauliflower rice. Like Kim Holderness, I lust after Target and cried against rain-covered windows during Covid when I wasn't making my weekly Target run. I used to joke that between 9am and 11am on any given weekday, you will see every mom with one kid (away in preschool) and a baby in their shopping cart wandering the Target aisles. With a Starbucks Coffee cup. I watch and laugh and share because in our relatability I can feel seen. My sameness and predictability makes me feel I am part of a good crowd. Not the popular crowd, but a majority online, at least. Among my similar demographic, at least.

Memes are funny because they are true about a lot of people. We see ourselves in them, or we send them to our friends when we recognize them in the witty words or images. While we may not watch the same TV shows every week thanks to streaming and other modern weirdness, the Internet is all the same. Memes and more reflect us back to ourselves. In a moment where we may feel divided and distant, we can share laughter at our own expense. Sharing in the joke helps us feel connected across a very broad world.

Me: IRL (In Real Life) may not be unique, but I'm pretty awesome. Hang on, I'll send you the meme to prove it.

SPILLED

I love a reusable cup. I feel so smug and environmental carrying around my coffee travel mug or Tervis for water or any other beverage. I take a relaxed early morning wander with my girlfriend Mandy twice a week. Six a.m. is the easiest availability in our hectic days so one of us pours coffee into travel mugs and we head out. It is usually her coffee. She is rich in delectable pour over coffee and so it is usually her pouring for us. Once in awhile I offer and she generously accepts my more traditional brew methods. Coffee is pretty great unless you work really hard to ruin it.

I grabbed two one-dollar reusable Starbucks cups...the ones that cost $1 and look just like their disposable cups. Usually I have a more substantial, sealed travel mug, but this morning these cups felt right. They were wrong. They were thin and I didn't have practical sleeves for them. I corralled the hot cups and the dog's leash heading out to walk the one block to meet Mandy. Cassie the dog decided to take care of business much earlier than usual. I still juggled the two cups and tried to enjoy the gorgeous orange and raspberry sunrise creeping up. The pup finished and I managed to take care of the situation without spilling a drop, but my early morning mood began to darken.

I greeted my pal who waited at the sidewalk for us and handed her a coffee cup. I was warning her it was thin & hot when I threw my cup to the ground. Not on purpose, but I still do not know what on Earth happened. I can balance and juggle when overextended, but then when all is simplified, I botch it? I was so pissed. I really want and need that morning cuppa.

Mandy offered her unscathed cup to me and I said, "No...you keep it!" and chucked my empty cup on the ground in anger. We stood there for a few beats and I sighed, picked it up and set it upright on the ground where I planned to leave it while we walked.

"Here, let's share this one." my friend said. She worked to open her lid and gestured to my empty vessel. "We can share it and it will cool off faster." It was such a good idea! Where had my brain been? Of course, I tried to say no, that she should enjoy the cup, but sharing prevailed and we split hers.

She took good care of me. It was a simple thing. I would have reacted the same way if roles were reversed. Why did I try to refuse her? Why would I have offered similar care to a friend but attempted to refuse accepting that same care? (It was just half a cup of coffee, after all!) It is more than a cup of coffee, after all.

I am not nice to myself. Sure, I give myself tasty treats and get my nails done, but I am not kind or generous. With my inner self I am more like the snowplow parent removing all difficulties from life. I make excuses, I am self-deprecating. I lavishly compliment others because I desperately need to hear the same kind words myself. I feel trapped and stuck inside my poor habit. I give reasonable reasons for any of my failings in the moment, with an audience. BUT when I get myself home, I am in trouble for them. I would sacrificially take coffee from my own cup for a friend but cannot easily accept the same in return.

I've been a horrid grouch lately. I know it is stress and uncertainty and weight gain. I know how to feel better, do better but I marinate in it all instead. I'm reading The Artist's Way by Julia Cameron about unleashing creativity, and I am taking workshops and I am trying to turn it around. I am learning to be aware of what could be underneath my initial reactions. I am channeling my inner artist, my inner child into all sorts of activities and exercises to live a better life. I don't have time to train wreck even one hour of my day when something spills. The good work on Earth needs to get done. Not everyone is built like me to encourage, challenge and break through the piles of muck. When I am kind to myself, I can be more loving to others throughout my day. I want to spill out all the goodness I can and share a view of sherbet sunrises for all to see. The only thing I want to spill out of my cup is encouragement. Shall we walk?

USED CARS

The worst job I ever had was also the most useful job I ever had. I've always enjoyed talking to people. My ability to engage and connect makes me a natural for any customer focused sales position. My acting chops and outgoing, upbeat personality led me many different places to train and be trained for sales and customer service over the decades. For two months, that one time, it was on a Used Car Lot. I learned some things on the car lot which are helpful to remember when buying a car. I have used my car lot life lessons to sharpen many sales teams in a variety of industries!

My work at the dealership was short lived. You see, I preferred the customer to The Deal, so instead of trying to get them to pay as much as possible, I tried to shave and wheedle prices down so far that my bosses had to have The Talk with me. I was encouraged to upsell, upcharge, etc. to earn a higher margin for my own paycheck.   I learned that the F&I Guy would be able to insert other fees...especially for those of you who lease a car. Dave Ramsey calls 'leasing' 'fleecing' and I do not think he is wrong. I felt uncomfortable and awkward and I did have trouble memorizing boring car details and numbers for the required '6 point walk around'. I tried to quit the first month.

They insisted I stay. I guess they saw the diamond in the rough I could be as a used car salesperson. I wasn't intimidated by the Boys Club. I was fun to work with. I even had a pink and blue plaid sport coat I wore ironically. I loved people but hated the pounce.... I've chuckled with my daughters and demonstrated the feral way salespeople will stalk and pounce on you when driving onto a car lot. They erupted with giggles when we drove on and then back off a lot, pursued hotly by eager sales folks. I don't mean to mock every salesperson...remember, I am one too! But good guys in the used car arena are a rare find.

I met a Stellar Salesman the last time I bought a car. After two weeks of exhaustive car shopping and fitfully sleepless nights, I met Joe Orosz Jr. He was only the second of seven car salesmen I talked to and liked. The poor thing and his wife had six-year-old triplet girls and their 8yo big sister to manage. I am pretty sure his wife is a saint. Anyway, he and I had witty banter and I was very direct with him about what we wanted, what we could afford and that we were paying cash, Dave Ramsey style.

I was floored when Joe offered to drive the Honda Pilot to my house for the test drive! This man understood having small children. Later, when Joe stuck out his finger for my baby daughter to grab for a big stair step I quipped,

"Look at all those cars being sold! Right now, as we stand here, cars are flying right off this lot!" As funny as it was and as cheesy as it could have been, I believed him. Maybe he only plays video games at home and belches beer when he asks his saintly wife to bring him a sammich, but I saw Joe as a charming family man. Well played or real, I hope I never know.

When buying cars, I want to feel like I got a great deal. My deal was so good I am not sharing the details! I might have even gotten Joe to dance on a desk to close the deal. If you find him now at Paul Huering Ford, let him know that you know he dances on the desk! You won't even have to say Heather sent you.

Joe said always get the car checked out through your own mechanic before you buy. We do this and it costs only time and about $25 for peace of mind. Research online for YOUR car and the car you are looking at before you go see it. Aim for middle prices but expect to pay a bit more or receive a bit less. Your salesperson does intend to make a living, and they should. But. Never, Never, Never pay sticker (AKA 'Asking') price. NEVER. Even if it is a 'no haggle' lot like Carmax, ask them to sweeten the deal with services, extra keys, increasing your trade value or warranties. And Buy the car, no leasing. Don't ever lease a car. Leasing means you are paying extra to look wealthier than you are. (It hurts but It is true.)

Dealerships invest in cars as a business and want to make a profit, but, if you do your research, you can avoid accidentally paying for someone else's new yacht. Take along your most assertive, sales savvy friend and never be afraid to walk away from a car you feel iffy about. Now if you'll excuse me, l need to go see a man about a car.

ALMOST HAPPINESS

You have heard me complain before about laundry. I mean, everyone has heard almost everyone complain about some aspect of laundry. If you are in the family way, even if your offspring does their own laundry...they never really do their own laundry. Someone left socks on the floor of the garage and another pair in the hall. Someone else won't fold without a fight...especially if it is not their item. Even as the Mama I struggle to hold authority in the putting away of the washed, dried, folded clothes. It is true that a basket of perfectly completed laundry has sat at the foot of my bed long enough to get covered completely with far flung lightly used I'll hang it back up tomorrow is this smelly I guess I'll wash it all laundry.

Some of you sainted folk really enjoy laundry. Perhaps you have a pretty, Pinterest worthy laundry room. You may use all that delicious, scented laundry soap and you probably hum as you fold it all Marie Kondo style. My laundry resides in a serial killer influenced basement. I tried putting up cute sayings and pictures and still.... nah. The only thing that gets laundry done in my home is literal desperation and a gripping audiobook. Or having someone else do it instead of me.

I know I should be grateful. I know the laboriousness of lugging laundry to a laundromat. To sit amongst stranger's unmentionables and hope no prior customer dried crayons or lipsticks along with their toddler sized jammies. I've been to another country where the locals washed their clothing in mostly clean water and laid the pieces out to dry on dirt and grass. I know I should be grateful. I am mostly grateful to have too many clothes and enough physical health to do the dumb laundry. I know not everyone does. I'm grateful my life is so uneventful that I have little else to complain about. I do take some pleasure from prettily folded items filling up laundry baskets. Folded fabric that dreams to one day be carried upstairs to be put away at long last. I also recently found a new pleasure in making laundry even more difficult to complete!

My husband and I were in Nappanee to drop our kids at Lutherwald summer camp in Howe, Indiana. As we wandered from breakfast to woodshop to yard sale, I admired the Amish homes with laundry hanging outdoors on the line. Living in the area, I've dined at Amish homes, gone to Beekeeper Auctions with my Dad and ridden in horse drawn buggies. I never admired the laundry on the line. At my house we do have drying racks in the basement for laundry that needs extra care, but not a laundry line outdoors. For heaven's sake! How much harder could I make doing this despised chore?!? Lug a basket of wet laundry up a flight of stairs on top of the other steps? No way.

I kept thinking about the laundry outdoors on the line. We'd begun air drying more often to help the environment and try to save on our gas bill. I wondered if by making the laundry more difficult, I could take it more seriously. Could I enjoy some Laura Ingalls style living? I talked to my husband, John, and we agreed to try line drying outdoors for as long as our fickle Midwestern weather would allow. I bought a zippy retractable jobber and John installed it. I will say the first time was the best time. Handling each towel, each clothespin...was meditative. Being outside I felt smug and environmental and cool but also refreshed. Standing in the sunshine, hearing the sounds of my neighborhood and hanging damp clothes up was...pleasant.

The kids also enjoyed hanging their clothes outside...after grumbling about the cruelty and unfairness of it all first. I have forgotten laundry overnight...which then covered with dew needed to dry all over again. My husband didn't love the crunchy nature of his jeans, our towels.... but they settled down after a bit. Sometimes I run them through the dryer instead. I have started noticing others hanging laundry outside and I smile. I am in a club of sorts now. I still haven't discovered the sweet spot of a 'cycle' time; how long everything needs to dry out. Laundry that is folded still languishes in the baskets...but it smells fresh, like sunshine...almost like happiness.

CLEANING IS DANGEROUS

Do you have that thing in your house that desperately needs to be dealt with? The pile of debris or that stack of bins or the closet where you hide the bodies of unwanted houseguests? I had a few totes in the dining room for too long. We used them every week, but we didn't have a lot of space in there, so they inhibited our daily life. My husband was working from home one Friday afternoon and I gleefully addressed the totes, squared off, picked them up and headed to the basement where they belonged. As I sauntered past my darling hubby, I grinned widely and proudly declared that after MONTHS I was returning the eyesore to its rightful place in the basement.

I was unfortunately overconfident in my abilities. I apparently skipped a few crucial stairs on my way to the basement. My husband came running as totes went flying (one made it into the basement end over end down the stairs unaccompanied). I knelt awkwardly on the landing gasping in pain. I have always been clumsy and falling feels like a hobby at this point. I began to check myself out and knew I'd hurt my ankle, but then it all got fuzzy. John was there at my side, fortunately, as I went into shock. I'm not sure why that happened, but it was scary. He gently coaxed me along with his warm presence and a glass of water.

After a while I scootched on my butt back up the steps and to the couch to ice my ankle. As my leg changed shape and color, we decided x-rays were in order. We begged crutches off my sweet neighbor to avoid an ambulance ride. When all was said and done, I had a broken leg and needed surgical correction for damage around my ankle. I should have left the freakin' totes in the blankety blank dining room. The last time I broke my foot I was carrying a vacuum cleaner up the stairs. Cleaning is DANGEROUS. I do not recommend it.

I had to be completely off the leg for a hideously long time. About eight weeks. Now don't get me wrong, laying on the couch like the Queen of Sheba suits me just fine. For a few days. After that everyone in the house wants to start crying. I neighbor-sourced a knee scooter and moved into our downstairs sunroom/guestroom. My fashion choices centered on the boot, then the cast, and my energy level any given day. Sleeping in the clunky cast I named "Big Bertha" was crummy...moving was crummy...not moving was crummy.

I was whiny and demanding and couldn't drink my sorrows away because I had to be fully with it to move my body safely. Even sober and not cleaning the house I fell, tottering off the scooter, falling with crutches, hopping wrong and crashing on down to the floor. After the sixth time, my friends threatened to buckle me into a wheelchair. I didn't leave the house often. It was too hard, too scary. I was very grateful to stay home, to not have a job that needed me to show up on two legs. My friends made food, brought flowers, cleaned and sat beside me on the couch. I left the house with loving escorts so if (and when) I fell, help would be right there.

Now I am on the other side of the mountain. I can put weight on my ankle, but it isn't easy. I'm still using all the scooters and crutches and it is frustrating. Physical therapy is helpful but unpleasant. Even folks who love me most are likely tired of hearing "Hey, would you mind getting-me thatsockacupofcoffeemycrutchthebook?" and "While you are up, could you please refillthebirdfeedergetthedoorletthedoginhandme thatpillowrunthevaccum?" I'm sick of myself too. I feel guilty and foolish and there isn't much I can do about any of it. I say thank you A LOT. I've hired some folks to do some things to hopefully take the pressure off my friends & family. I have made too many purchases on Amazon. Again.

John brought me to one of my doctor appointments and I noticed a young woman in my situation. She had a Big Bertha Boot of her own and a walker. She was alone. I ache for folks doing this sort of thing all by themselves. I wonder if it is by choice or simply circumstance. Friends beside you make most things better. I hope that each of us has someone beside us for the hard times, and the good times too. Maybe you can even get them to carry your thing back to that place for you!

MODERN CIVILITY

My husband says he is a grumpy old man even though he is not old! He is a little bit of a cynic. While his loyalty runs deep to work, friends and of course, darling me, he rarely feels safe meeting new people. He's seen enough human behavior to know he wants to choose carefully how he spends his heart and time. I, on the other hand, am the Five Year Old. He likens me to that freckled girl in pigtails of my youth standing in the front yard addressing everyone passing by with "Hi! I'm Heather! Wanna be friends?!?" He's not wrong. I find people fascinating. I wade in during the first conversation asking about their sex lives and political views. I then hit any other awkward topics as an oversharer...all but inviting them to live with us starting next week.

I like living that way. I've tried to put a filter on it, but...well...Nope. I seize almost all of my days and the people wandering into them. I am the same person in my backyard, at church, in the store and standing on my front lawn hollering "Hi!" I am a 'what you see is what you get' (even if you don't really want it) person. BUT. I admit I have begun to understand my husband's view on people a bit better these most recent years.

I didn't know so many Americans were still racist. And sexist. And Angry. Until He that shall not be named showed up changing my America, I was blissfully ignorant. Sure I heard about things and read the news...I showed up at protests, volunteered and voted. I ran in circles of good people, even online, and I didn't realize that just because a person reached adulthood didn't mean they were grownup. At first I was sad when someone would bark at me in an online comment. I was unprepared for the nasty comments on other's comments from strangers on the internet.

I care about people, and I try to move through the world making that clear. Seeing people act so ugly towards each other hurts my soul. It hurts my faith in people and God. The reality that people have recently felt more emboldened to hate each other sucks. Any adult choosing to hate a whole group of people because of how they look, their religion or lack thereof, who they choose to love....are you kidding me? The distance of the computer keyboard affords immature people the option to be horrible, without facing the very real person they are being horrible to. I had to put my arms around that Little 5 year old Front Yard Heather, and explain that not all strangers are worthy of her warmth and friendship.

I can understand a person being raised to believe something, even something evil, will have a hard time trying to retrain their brain. If your whole family, whom you love deeply, think something, it would be near impossible to break from them by believing differently. When someone is ugly or cruel or judgmental, I remind myself how difficult it must be for them. I imagine the pain it must bring to live in this little box holding onto garbage, too afraid to admit it is just that. Of course they lash out in their desperation to be right. None of us ever want to be wrong.

What would help us now is modern civility. I miss the days I've never known where manners mattered enough that adults used them. I want to use my good manners with people. I apologize when I am wrong, and I am often wrong. I want to offer my best to the people I interact with. Even if they cannot do the same for me. (Although I wish they could do the same for me, and for you, too.) I believe adults should be civil even as they disagree with each other.

My Little Heather in the Front Yard has grown up the hard way these recent years. I do not like people as much, but I do understand my husband better. When people disappoint enough, you need to protect yourself. I'm glad to know the truth about the anger and hatred in my country, but I miss my innocence. Now that I live in this modern reality, I will do my best from my own front yard to model modern civility. I will take action for what is right. I'll create space for angry people to change into people with open hearts and minds and possibly some manners.

BLUE CHRISTMAS

I wish I could find the words to write novels. I love reading them so much! My writing skill set lies in short bites of life instead of ongoing plot twists and the heroine getting her man. This Holiday season I'm searching for the words to help my friends, family and myself. This year as I'm wrapping gifts and baking, I am not as cheerful as usual. I understand the concept of the phrase "Blue Christmas" differently, personally. I find myself with dear friends in hard places that will impact their holiday joy. My friend is battling cancer for the fourth ugly year. The family man who was in a tragic car accident and is now confined to a wheelchair. Their Christmases will still happen but could be shaded blue.

I find my own family feeling uncertain and sad as my dear Mother in Love struggles to recover from Covid and a host of health issues. I sit with her and reassure her that she has built an incredible family legacy. Yes, I will make your nut roll. Yes, we know you love us. She speaks of letters she wants to write to each of us, and I listen. We bring milkshakes and cute grandchildren and tabletop trees. We rearrange our traditions to avoid the undecorated house this year. The grandkids grumble, seeing only their perspective in the moment. Minutes later, they create beauty for Baba and bake and craft and pray for her health. We are afraid of losing her. She is afraid of leaving us, or of not leaving and being stuck in a body she cannot use. This colors the traditions for each of us a sorrowful blue.

My friend who cheerfully spends most of her time in chemotherapy or recovering from it still manages to smile. She offered to bring me anything I might want or need when I shared I was getting sick. I asked what thoughts she might have about Blue Christmas, about how she finds light even in darkness. She said "I try, like every day, to make the most out of what time I have here. It makes you realize life is too short. Put up the decorations, the tree, even if you don't have ornaments on it yet! Do what brings you the most joy." She said remembering their holiday traditions and sharing stories of the past helps bring laughter and joy even in sad times.

The family man who has had a lot taken from him this year still has a smile for his cute wife or video game advice for his growing boys. He weighs in on household life and makes sure his wife gets out of the house for weekly game nights and events to refresh her. He plays online games with his friends and allows all the people who love and enjoy him to move into his personal pain and space to build ramps, paint rooms, change out carpet for wheelchair friendly laminate. He wears his Star Wars shirts and snuggles his wife. I see all of this from a distance, and I am humbled. My time with his wife is mostly lighthearted. Despite her own family chaos, she is quick to offer help to all of us. Their faith in God is strong. If I asked her how she is keeping her holiday cheer this year, she would likely say something about her boys. She wants to give them a happy Christmas. Other people are her focus, even though her precious mom died only weeks after her husband's accident. She feels her pain fully, acknowledges the suck and then looks around to see what she can do now. What new story can she tell?

I think those are the words we need here: the way to keep holiday cheer sprinkled through a Blue Christmas is to take care of yourself. Acknowledge pain, fear or sorrow and find the small things to lift even our heavy spirits. Then, turn to others, help someone, anyone, else. I have looked for ways to do this for my own Blue Christmas. Visiting folks and bringing gifts. Extra snuggles with my daughters. Making plans (and with an impending blizzard, contingency plans!). I asked my family what is most important so we can hit at least the high points. I've been making many gifts with soft yarns, a crochet hook and my hands.

Some of us experiencing a Blue Christmas may just sit at home in a ball of blankets on the couch and that is 100% right in the moment. If this is you Dear One, consider sitting upright for only a moment, and lighting a candle for yourself. Even when we feel sorrow and darkness, there is always a tiny light. Sometimes we just must spark it ourselves. Please do.

POOL PEOPLE

Last week I dreamt that I awoke to a snow-covered yard. I know, it is now June and these fears should be far behind me, but the seasons have been discombobulated. We need to admit snow in June might not be completely off the table. On the subject of hell freezing over, despite my aversion to our hot, humid Indiana summers, I have found a secret to change my mind. Yes folks, despite the 100% likelihood that five minutes outdoors after ten in the morning will coat me in rivulets of sweat, I love it. Of course, you are on the edge of your hot, sticky lawn chairs to hear why, right? My secret is the grown up answer to the kiddie pool!

Last year our pandemic plan was hunker down and wait. Asking two rambunctious kids to stay home from the beach and camp and playgrounds was not a fun prospect, so we bought them a pool. We have a tiny yard, so we needed a tiny pool. And with my sharp wit, we couldn't risk one of those inflatable jobbers....we needed a miniature above ground pool of serious construction. After heated competition on ebay while everyone else had the same great idea, we landed an eight foot "Summer Waves" frame pool.

We told the kids, stalked the tracking number and at last it arrived. We smoothed down the area where we wanted our pool, removed stones and plants and added sand. We followed directions and put that baby together and started filling it up. It took awhile. Like hours and hours. I think we all got in it when it only had a few inches of water. We became "Pool People". We bought chlorine, floats, and more beach towels. We started sweeping the patio area more often. We wandered outdoors to just take a little dip. We added an outdoor speaker. We bought more ice pops and plastic cups. Mama bought a lounger that came with a cup holder...then bought another for The Daddy. While the pool was for the kids, I often staked a claim to float solo or with another adult. Two loungers fit, no more. And no kids. I unapologetically took over my kid's pool regularly.

I have rediscovered summer. I am having a new childhood outdoors despite the heat. I welcome the humidity. I have found that after a dip in the chilly little pool I can do a bit of yard work. I refill bird feeders and hang up wet towels. With the speaker blasting Beastie Boys and David Bowie and New Order, I am watering the outdoor pots more often. They might not die this year. I am enjoying my hammock more and when I do feel hot and sweaty...I plunge into the tiny pool. It is luscious and refreshing. I enjoy running the skimmer through it 238 times a day. This summer I got more pool treatments to keep it clean and clear since we have more company. My kid's friends show up at our gate with a towel over their shoulder and we have snacks to bring out poolside.

My six foot four Dad loves to plop his gangly self down into the pool when he visits. And of course, there must be a cocktail provided. I lure my friends to hang out with me with the offer of the adult floatie and a tiki cup filled with ice and sweetness. For a few moments, we stop adulting and ignore life's responsibilities and bask in childhood relived. I enjoy playing with my kids in the pool, too. They play "Pretend to skim the pool" and "Forget to rinse your feet before stepping in " and "Splash mom but get mad if she splashes back". I kind of like those games anyway. It is hard to be grouchy in a pool. Our tiny pool is the perfect answer to sweaty, humid, summer weather. We do not have to go on a road trip, rent a place or even drive to the beach to relax and cool off. We simply step out our back door into our own private oasis.

RITUALLY SPEAKING

My Unitarian upbringing is filtering through my consciousness and I find myself questing spiritually once again. I talked with a witchy friend about her craft with deep curiosity and openness. My fascination with energy medicine, crystals and incense feels more spiritual and downright witchy compared to my church's Sunday services. I discovered the word for 'witch' actually meant 'wise'. I considered the witch hunts in patriarchal societies where men in power were afraid of losing that power. It feels painfully familiar in this day and age. I've been reading, talking and learning about the power of energy, intent and words. I've been learning a lot about habits, rituals, and why we do what we do the way we do.

Jewish Shabbat candles on Friday nights, Pagan candle magic, Lutheran candles and rites and repeat after me's...they are beautiful rituals. In our family, being served cake in bed on the morning of your birthday is a whole thing. God help me if I serve anything but pizza for Friday Night Pizza and a movie with the family. Many people have a strong tradition, a ritual, of a big

Sunday Dinner. Some of us take tea or coffee drinking to a ritual. French press or scheduled coffee maker...whole beans only and at least two pushups against the counter while waiting for the coffee maker to finish.

According to Wikipedia, a ritual has four dimensions: content, frequency, intensity, and centrality. They can be characterized by traditionalism, symbolism, and performance. Ari Shapiro recently interviewed author Dimitri Xygalatas about his book "Ritual: How Seemingly Senseless Acts Make Life Worth Living" he said ,"Rituals are important to human life... even when they help individuals, through their anxieties, connect to one another." I thought that was curious...the idea of ritual being connected to anxiety. I myself am not an anxious person. I have heard of folks who have to check their locks or something similar a certain way or amount of times....a compulsion but also a bit of a ritual. Outside of church attendance my only ritual acts I'd been aware of were binging whatever I watched on Netflix or napping in the afternoon.

I balk at anything like rules or "must dos' ' but I do admire ritual from afar. When I found out I was 1% Jewish from a DNA test, I tried to make a Friday night Shabbat happen...because I liked the candlelight. The other 99% of me got in the way. Instead, I asked myself what I liked about that ritual. It was the dark night warmed by candlelight. I liked the weekly ritual and invitation to slow down shared by family. I realized I could make my own ritual instead of appropriating another culture's. While my family isn't quite on board yet, I have begun lighting candles on Sundays (or Mondays!) to welcome the evening. I often light candles in the morning to give our home that soft sweetness in an otherwise busy morning.

I covet the ritual of a daily walk. (I'm pretty sure my poor doggo does too!) I haven't made that new habit, that life affirming ritual happen yet. We are sporadic and it is always wonderful! Walking in the neighborhood I see things more slowly than when I zoom through in the car. It takes me longer to move through the spaces and places, but it also calms me and helps me take better care of my sweet pet. I like the idea of long daily walks, but do not know how to make them not just a habit, but a real ritual for myself. Unlike many rituals, there is no group with me to keep me following along.

Considering possibility in my daily life has led me to take many of the small things more seriously. I've begun giving thanks for all the hands along the food production line when I eat a meal. I'm lighting candles more often. I've been putting down my phone a little more and watching the tiny interactions available to me. As I seek more magic in my life, I can see the value in everything. Recognizing life through small rituals makes me more aware and present to the whole wide world. In making space for ritual in daily life, I discover more life in my days.

CHICAGO DREAMS

On my early morning walk with my friend Mandy, I lamented my inaction in getting the family to Chicago for Christmas. I enjoyed the Marshall Field windows and Barney's display when I lived there. The oversized everything. Year after year I imagine the glorious visage of the Mag Mile, a mere one hour drive away. I mentally plan to take my daughters and husband into the belly of the city for frivolity. And we do not go. I am not good at planning actual adventures, and wrangling a family of four to face the same direction for any activity is nightmarish to me. Our home is comfy and we all find good things to do and so we do not head out into the unknown often.

My friend Mandy asked if I wanted to go to Chicago with her instead. She painted a day of Ramen, gorgeous ice cream and of course thrif– antiquing. She is a pastor and professor and able to carve a fun day out of her schedule only on rare occasions. I began to salivate, and then confessed the only weekday I have off is Tuesday. Tuesdays are for visiting Monte, my Mother in Love. She lives in a fancy rehab community in Dyer an hour away, so spending time with her for lunch, Gin Rummy and gossip is a four hour deal. Mandy suggested we take her with us to Chicago. I began to protest that she wouldn't want to bother, that it would be too complicated medically and logistically as she is in a wheelchair.

Mandy talked of sliding Monte's wheelchair into the back of my minivan on homemade rails. We drove into the city and to a ramen place she knows. We slurp hot, steamy, noodles and crunch al dente vegetables in spicy broth. We use so many napkins. We planned to take a gummy since it is legal there and of course we give one to Monte for her aches and pains. In our adventures we only have to unload her once and she enjoys this wild deviation from reality. We head to a perfect ice cream shop as the munchies roll in, and we drool over all the options for mix-ins and flavors and we all order too much of a good thing. We sit around a tiny parlor table and spoon cold, creamy goodness into our mouths. We talk and giggle like middleschool girls until we cannot breathe. The staff begins to side eye the three of us, and we laugh even harder. Afterwards, we wander through the cutest shops with open ADA doorways, generous budgets and then, Monte, high as a kite, reminds me she wants to ice skate.

When she speaks of Heaven, Monte will be ice skating or riding her bike. She will be healthy and whole and free. So we head to Maggie Daley Park, to the ice skating ribbon there that weaves in and out and around in a never ending loop. Even though I am clumsy and fat and scared, this time I lace up skates with glee. My dear Mother in Love rises from the wheelchair once her ice skates are on and the years melt away. She looks radiant with hope and as beautiful as ever. Monte, Mandy and I hit the ice with all the grace of Olympic athletes. The cold winter air sparkles with magic and fluffy snowflakes drift down onto our faces. The blades of our skates scrape and carve the ice, pressing us forward. Our cheeks grow rosy with the cold and the tips of our fingers are a little numb. Our hearts soar as we skate easily across the ice. We glide, swirl and twirl together around the skating ribbon path. Monte ends up ahead of us, gliding peacefully with pure joy on her face. She giggles like a young girl and pulls ahead of us, rounding the bend. When we turn the corner she is gone.

BIBLIOGRAPHY

Cilley, Marla. The Fly Lady
https://flylady.net

Eldredge, John, and Eldredge, Stasi. (2005)
Captivating: Unveiling the Mystery of a Woman's
Soul
https://wildatheart.org/
Nelson Books

Food Network Kitchens. (April 2020) Food
Network Magazine the Big, Fun Kids Cookbook:
150+ Recipes for Young Chefs
Hearst Home Kids

Geocaching.com
https://www.geocaching.com/play

Hollis, Rachel.(October 2018) Girl, Wash Your Face
Nelson Books
https://msrachelhollis.com/

Kondo, Marie (October 2014) The Life-Changing
Magic of Tidying Up: The Japanese Art of

Decluttering and Organizing
Ten Speed Press
https://konmari.com/

Konkoly, Steven. (December 14, 2014) The Jakarta
Pandemic: A Post-Apocalyptic Survival Thriller
Stribling Media

Lamott, Anne (2000) Travelling Mercies, Some
Thoughts on Faith
Anchor

Leake, Lisa. 100 Days of Real Food
https://www.100daysofrealfood.com/

McCloud, Cathay (October 15, 2007) Have You
Filled A Bucket Today? A Guide for Daily Happiness
for Kids
Fearne Press

Miller, Don.(2009) Blue Like Jazz
Thomas Nelson

Precourt, Stephanie. Adventures in Babywearing
http://www.adventuresinbabywearing.com/

Ross, Melody. Brave Girls Club
https://melodyrossmedia.com/

Rubin, Gretchen.(December 2009) The Happiness

Project: Or, Why I Spent a Year Trying to Sing in the Morning, Clean My Closets, Fight Right, Read Aristotle, and Generally Have More Fun
Harper

Stanley, Andy. Taking Responsibility for Your Life Group Bible Study by Andy Stanley
https://youtu.be/_HQzMYI9UfI
Zondervan

Terkeurst, Lysa, (January 2011) Made to Crave: Satisfying Your Deepest Desire with God, Not Food
Harper Christian

Turner, Jessica. (June 23, 2014) Moms, Put on That Swimsuit
https://www.huffpost.com/entry/moms-put-on-that-swimsuit_b_5521937
Huffington Post

US Department of Homeland Security
https://www.ready.gov/

"Various Heather Curlee Novak Essays" Michiana Chronicles WVPE 88.1 2009-2023

Xygalatas, Dimitris. (September 2022) Ritual: How Seemingly Senseless Acts Make Life Worth Living
Little, Brown Spark

AFTERWORD

Through all of these words I hope to show you options for an imperfect life, well-lived. I hope my musings invite you to share your own life stories with me and your people. I am still fumbling towards my best life, and you may know some things I'd like to hear!

Reach out to HeatherCurleeNovak@gmail.com
or www.HeatherCurleeNovak.com
and tell me all about your life.

Follow me on Instagram @HeatherCurleeNovak
for my "Hi Friend!" posts.

Read my other books:
Heather Curlee Novak Author Amazon Page

ABOUT THE AUTHOR

Heather Curlee Novak

 Heather is a woman who knows red lipstick and glitter are for more than special occasions. She has lived a lot of life--some of it messy, most of it meaningful--and she is eager to help other folks find energy, engagement, and excitement in their stories.

Heather is happily married to her personal Prince Charming, John, and they have two fascinating daughters they encourage to live well.

Heather's professional history includes customer service, sales training, and troubleshooting, but she loves motivational speaking the best. Heather lives each day as if it were her last and strives to live her love out loud.

Made in the USA
Monee, IL
14 November 2024

70153276R00154